My Vanishing
Country

My Vanishing Country

A MEMOIR

Bakari Sellers

AMISTAD

An Imprint of HarperCollins*Publishers*

FIRST EDITION

Designed by Terry McGrath

Library of Congress Cataloging-in-Publication Data

Names: Sellers, Bakari, 1984– author.
Title: My vanishing country : a memoir / Bakari Sellers.
Description: First edition. | New York, NY : Amistad, 2020
Identifiers: LCCN 2019040021 | ISBN 9780062917454 (hardcover) | ISBN 9780062917461 (paperback) | ISBN 9780062940315 (ebook) | ISBN 9780062917478 (ebook)
Subjects: LCSH: Sellers, Bakari, 1984– | African American legislators—South Carolina—Biography. | Legislators—South Carolina—Biography. | South Carolina. General Assembly. House of Representatives—Biography. | Rural African Americans—South Carolina—Social conditions—20th century. | Racism—South Carolina—History—21st century. | Denmark (S.C.)—Biography.
Classification: LCC F275.42.S45 A3 2020 | DDC 328.73/092 [B]—dc23
LC record available at https://lccn.loc.gov/2019040021

20 21 22 23 24 LSC 10 9 8 7 6 5 4 3 2 1

For Ellen, Kai, Stokely, and Sadie

God of our weary years
God of our silent tears
Thou who has brought us thus far on the way
Thou who has by thy might
Led us into the light
Keep us forever in the path, we pray

—"Lift Every Voice and Sing,"
J. Rosamond Johnson and James Weldon Johnson

CONTENTS

My Vanishing
Country

Black, Country, and Proud

I'm from what's called the Low Country in South Carolina, where beauty and blight and history are intertwined. You can drive for fifty miles in any direction and still be on the same grounds where slaves, some of them my not-so-distant ancestors, toiled over cotton, indigo, sugarcane, rice, wheatgrass, and soybeans. Particularly, my hometown is Denmark, South Carolina—a place where everybody knew my last name, a name, I would learn as a child, that was colored with honor and infamy.

To get to Denmark, which is in Bamberg County, just drive down Highway 321 if you're coming from Columbia, the state capital. You'll pass fields of corn and cotton and flash by acres of swampland creeping over neon-green beds of marsh.

You'll eventually seem to arrive halfway around the globe

in a little slice of "Scandinavia," where towns dubbed Norway, Sweden, and finally Denmark appear one after another. The first two are so teeny, you'll miss them if you blink. Before them, you'll tick past a chicken farm that always smells of pure shit before you eventually get to Denmark, a community of thirty-four hundred souls, nearly all African American.

Visitors often think that the "Scandinavian" towns, which are nine miles apart from each other, are so called because of Nordic settlers, but that's not so. The monikers actually followed that theme only when my hometown was named after B. A. Denmark, a nineteenth-century railroad businessman.

I always liked to imagine my own alternative theory: that my town was tagged after a badass freed and literate African-American carpenter named Denmark Vesey, who was convicted and executed for leading "the rising," a deftly plotted slave revolt in 1822. Vesey's sense of justice and his rebellious nature have always appealed to me.

Continuing through those isolated hamlets, you'll pass graceful Victorians and dilapidated shotgun houses. They say a bullet can fly from the front door straight through the back door of these narrow dwellings, which is how we once believed the shotguns got their names. But a growing theory is that the name of these skinny homes, which are no more than twelve feet wide, comes from a style of house in West Africa called *shogun*, which means God's house. The shotguns play a huge role in southern history and African-American folklore in the deep parts of the South, as do the abandoned buildings that make up the dying downtowns.

To me, there's a rustic beauty to ghost towns, with their ramshackle clues of a fruitful past. The empty downtowns conjure feelings of nostalgia and sorrow simultaneously: in Denmark, I can drive up to a gas station and see a man from childhood standing outside, and I realize that same man has been standing around there for twenty-some years.

Denmark is an intriguing country town, especially when you consider what it has to offer, or all it used to be. It's about an hour from Augusta, Charleston, and Columbia, and thanks to old B. A., it was once a transportation hub, with trains from three large train companies coming and going. Once bustling, Denmark's downtown today is the perfect example of what's happening in the forgotten rural Black Belt, a term once used to label a section of the country known for its dark, rich soil. Now, however, it describes a chain of connecting states known as the nation's largest contiguous thread of poverty.

Most of the businesses that were open in Denmark in my father's day are now shuttered. A Laundromat is still open, as well as Poole's Five and Dime, a few restaurants, and a hardware store—but that's nearly it. The entire area no longer has a hospital. Whether it's Denmark or somewhere else in Alabama or Mississippi, if you had driven through forty years ago, it would have been pulsing with energy and black life. The train tracks traveled north, south, east, and west, heading to Chicago, Atlanta, New York City, and Los Angeles. At one time, Denmark had a pickle factory, a Coca-Cola bottling plant, and a furniture manufacturing company. The town was packed with people of all trades—bricklayers, technicians, construction workers, bakers, painters, and cooks—as well as black businesses of every kind, which is why you had some wealth in a place that's 85 percent black.

Despite today's extreme poverty in my hometown, significant numbers of educated black people have always lived in Denmark, especially since two historically black colleges are located there: Denmark Technical College and Voorhees College, where my father was president. All these things were going for it, but when the tracks got pulled up, politics blew in. People talk about corporations coming in and destroying towns, but I believe that South Carolina was devastated by the 1994 North American Free Trade Agreement (NAFTA). The textile mills started closing their doors and moving overseas, people started leaving, and with them, all the jobs vanished.

• •

In 1990, when I was six years old, my father moved our family from Greensboro, North Carolina, back to his hometown of Denmark, from which he had fled more than twenty years earlier. He was the city's prodigal son coming home. If I had been older, our move to this black, rural outpost would have given me pause, but the very thing I should have been wary about is the thing my six-year-old self loved most: everybody knew our name.

In South Carolina, black folk don't ask each other's last name; we ask about kin. And, of course, there are many versions of this custom, depending on where you're from. For instance, African Americans in the state's Upcountry might say, "What's your people's name?" In Denmark, it's "Who's your people?" It's a very direct question to determine who's someone's mother and father and any other relative one might need to know. It helps us to determine whether we're blood and possibly even more. It reveals our lineage and background.

The custom can easily be traced back to slavery. Slaves were separated from their loved ones and stripped of everything they held dear. So now, we're left always searching for a kindred spirit, grasping for home, which is why we call each other "cousin" or "uncle" or "aunt" or "sis," even when we're not blood-related.

As a reluctant little boy moving to a new town, I quickly realized Denmark wasn't unfamiliar territory. Everywhere I turned, someone, child or adult, was telling me, "We're your kin," or "You Bakari . . . Cleveland Sellers' boy!," or "You Little CL," or "I knew your granddaddy!"

Denmark was where my roots were planted.

It's home.

• •

Driving through Denmark's desolate downtown is like looking into a loved one's eyes and no longer seeing a twinkle. The light has dimmed. What once was a sparkle, is no longer.

Denmark is a microcosm of the forgotten black South, where isolation, lack of economic development, and substandard housing and school systems have devastated it to its core. What I've seen all my life in Denmark helped me to cultivate my political belief that small businesses are the lifeblood of all communities. Whether you look back at Tulsa's wealthy "Black Wall Street" of the early twentieth century or the Harlem Renaissance of the 1920s or the Sellers family in Denmark circa 1950s and 1960s, black people and black power always meant being able to have economic self-sustainability and access to the ballot box.

However, you can see in poor black towns today that international industry and a globalized economy have left most of us behind. Denmark is now a place where no one can take for granted things such as clean water, a simple Wi-Fi connection, and a local hospital.

A Country Boy's Wonderful Life

By the time my family arrived in Denmark, my father had already received a graduate degree from Harvard University. Unfortunately, a prison record kept him from getting jobs he deserved.

Back in Greensboro, we had lived a strange existence, sometimes eating government food but also sometimes employing a maid. My parents struggled financially but wanted their children to live their best lives. For instance, my father has always been a staunch supporter of historically black colleges. Although he couldn't afford it, he'd take us to the colorful and famous North Carolina A&T football games, known for their marching bands and drumline. My sister tells the story of Daddy allowing us to walk onto the field with the marching band. Who'd suspect such adorable little kids were up to no good? Then we'd scamper into the stands where he had told us to meet him. It was a brilliant scheme and saved my father lots of money he didn't have; it also allowed us to have the time of our lives. We sat in the best seats, moving only when someone told us to get up from their spots, and then we'd just scoot over to some nearby empty ones. Our family made do, and me and my brother and sister rolled with it. When the electrical company shut our lights off, we just thought it was game night because we always played Monopoly in candlelight.

In 1990, my grandmother had just died of breast cancer in Denmark, and my grandfather had died a year earlier from pancreatic cancer. So we moved back to South Carolina into their home, a small ranch-sized house where my father had been raised. The bedrooms were lined up behind each other. First was my parents' room, which was connected to a door that led to my bedroom, and in my room was a door that opened into my older brother's room. My grandparents, who both had been quite ill before their deaths, didn't sleep together, which meant me and my brother were not only in their beds, but we were basically sleeping on their mattresses—their death beds. My brother thought it was especially "creepy" to sleep in granddaddy's bed because it's actually where he died.

My parents tried to make a living running the family motel next door. We also had property throughout the neighborhood and the area, property we still own. It was hard to get rent from people who couldn't always pay. We'd never kick them out but would take forty dollars here and fifty there. It was far more important to my father to help people keep their dignity than to take their money. However, we made more rent money when my father was in Africa for a few weeks and my mother was collecting rent. Everyone knew that Gwen Sellers did not play.

My mother, who's from Memphis, had a love-hate relationship with Denmark. She'd eventually love it after so many years, but she never liked it. Early on, she warned us that Denmark was backwards and that people wouldn't like us because of my father's past. She often discussed the difference between "country" and "southern," and she believed my father was "country," like Denmark.

My older sister, who was headed to college and wanted nothing to do with rural Denmark, was not country. I, on the other hand, embraced being "country," like Daddy. Right away, I loved Denmark. They say you can't squeeze blood from a turnip, but I did. What we didn't have, didn't matter. I squeezed everything I could get out of that old town. I took to the country vernacular, the pockmarked back roads, the ponds and the cotton fields where we played.

My brother, on the other hand, Cleveland Lumumba Sellers, who is eight years older than me, cried for two weeks after we left Greensboro. He wanted me to have a better experience adjusting, so he spent loads of time outside with me playing football or toss-up tackle (you throw the ball up in the air and whoever catches it runs until he gets tackled). We also went pole fishing in Mill Pond. Country folk have no need for reels or fancy gadgets we could never afford. We simply used an old cane pole, a line, and wigglers or worms from the corner store.

A good day of fishing is measured by the pain in your legs because that meant you were too busy to get up from the bucket you'd been sitting on. You'd also know you had a very good day if you left with that bucket filled with crappie, a bony fish that travels in pools. Crappies are easy to cook: you clean them, cover them with Lawry's Seasoned Salt, drop them in grease, and eat them with mustard and white bread. White bread was a staple in every house in Denmark because it was cheap. It also can stick to the roof of your mouth, but if a fish bone gets stuck in your throat, country folk know all you do is swallow a wad of white bread whole, which pushes the offending bone downward.

In Denmark, we rode bikes or walked everywhere. There was no "your friend's mom is about to pick you up" in the car. Our feet carried us where we needed to go.

Now in a rural town like Denmark, basketball was everything. On the weekends we'd literally break into the college gym, the same gym my daddy played in when he was a boy, until the coach found out and just unlocked the door for us. There were only two other basketball hoops in our area. One belonged to my friends Boo and Chicko, who lived in a house at the end of a street, and the other belonged to my family. It was located behind the family motel. We'd play so long and I'd get so dirty that my mother would make me undress outside the screen door.

But although I'd reach six-foot-five by age fifteen, I was no LeBron James. One of my best friends constantly told me how mediocre I was at basketball. His name was Jamil Williams, but we called him Pop. My family loved Pop. My father was like a surrogate parent to Pop, and he was like my brother. He was sweet-hearted but always in trouble. Pop was also a superb athlete. He ran track and was excellent at soccer and basketball. I, on the other hand, could tell you every statistic about my favorite players and teams, but I wasn't the most graceful athlete. Pop and I would sit in my room and talk about our favorite players. I would try to shoot hoops like my hero Larry Davis, a player from Denmark, but Pop always checked me. He'd shake his head, and in the most black country voice you could ever imagine, proclaim, "Bo"—which country folk say instead of "boy"—"Bo, gimme the ball. You can't play no ball, big head."

I'd say, "What you mean?"

"Just stick with the books," he'd say.

"You can't tell me I can't play," I'd say.

"Nah, you can shoot, but you have no hops."

Pop saw himself as my protector. He often said people thought the Sellers family had more than they did because most in town had nothing. "So, they took it as an opportunity to try to hurt Bakari," he'd tell people. "I'd step in and say 'You bednot! You ain't gonna lay a hand on Bakari!' And they didn't."

Pop was good for me. He introduced me to Denmark, to my new neighborhood, and showed me his life, which was very different from my own. He lived on "the other side of the tracks," the very rough side of town. First, you have to understand that the neighborhood I lived in was no prize; in fact, to outsiders it would look extremely desolate, a picture of poverty packed with abandoned shacks. But it was quiet, and every person knew every other person. There was an art studio across the street. We'd get penny candy from Mr. Meyers, a retired black businessman who'd park a chair in front of the store and fall asleep. Sometimes his sons would cook up hotdogs and sell them to us for pennies. The "Icy Lady" sold ice-cold slushies (frozen Kool-Aid in a Dixie cup) from her house. Even today, if my daddy leaves his keys in the truck, and someone takes the truck, someone else will knock on his door and return the keys.

But Pop's part of town was hard and sometimes violent. And though I wasn't particularly popular, I immediately became a cool kid because I knew people from both sides of the tracks.

The Boy with an Old Soul

My big brother Lumumba didn't have as easy a time adjusting to Denmark as I did. In fact, he was miserable, but he was also very practical, so he kept himself extremely involved in sports at the high school. I'd visit him in the locker room, which had no lights, so my brother's basketball team had to get dressed in the classroom before games. They had no warm-up suits, only shorts, but not enough for everyone, so every week one boy didn't get to play.

Pop and I traveled with him to other schools that had shiny gymnasiums and big, well-lit locker rooms. Although I was only six or seven, I'd wonder out loud why my brother's team could be treated this way when they were ranked as one of the best basketball teams in the nation.

Some may think that's a precocious thing for a child to say, but let me provide some context. Before we moved to Denmark, my father was taking prekindergarten me along to various community meetings and academic conferences. So, thanks to him, my brother, and Pop, I was developing a certain cultural awareness, an ability to understand my surroundings before I knew everything that was going on. The fact that Pop lived on one side of the tracks and we lived on the other was suddenly irrelevant: we were all struggling. And the disparities between my brother's dilapidated school and the rich white high schools he played against were clear as day.

Not everyone realized or appreciated this about me. Nosizwe, my sister, who is twelve years older than me, thought I was the strangest child in the world. "Bakari's not a normal child," she'd say. "He's a little old man in a child's body."

She'd tell my father, "I don't much like him."

"He's your little brother," my father would say. "You have to be nice to him."

I might have seemed like an old man at times to my sister, but I was also a child, with immature boyish ways. My family will be the first to say that no one could tell me what I couldn't do. And I freely admit, for one thing, I'm a crier like my dad. I get emotional and passionate about what I like, and what I believe I can do, and upset when I feel life is unjust or when something terrible happens to good people.

When I was eight, Duke University, my favorite team, lost the NCAA Division Regional final to Kentucky. I cut a fool. My family won't let me forget how I sprawled out on the floor of our den and screamed like someone was beating me. When my recreation basketball team lost in middle school, I lay out in the center of the gym, in front of everybody, screaming and crying and proclaiming we lost because the team was so horrible.

I could be just as passionate about justice and right and wrong. Pop often tells people, "Bakari, even as a little boy, was a slick talker. He'd debate anybody. I told him he was going to be a lawyer, or a politician, and he became both. Bakari would debate people on 'Why you want to fight that person? They didn't do anything to you.'"

Nosizwe saw me not as a lawyer in training but as a hyper-articulate and overly confident child, but I was also filled with anxiety, which makes for an odd character to both children and adults. Nosizwe and I had funny arguments about who was smarter. I think she wanted to try to prevent me from growing arrogant, though she was really not equipped to know how to do that. She'd say, "There's a fine line between confidence and arrogance. We both came from the same mama and daddy, and they taught us to do the same things. Whatever you can do, I can do too. I just chose in this world to be something else."

My smart mouth annoyed Nosizwe to no end, though we eventually became, and to this day still are, very close. And despite her initial irritation, my sister was like a second mother to me. When she was in medical school, most weekends she'd drive the ninety miles from Charleston to Denmark to come get me. I'd hang with her, talk to her girlfriends, eat at fancy restaurants, and go with her on dates. I called her "my mother-sister-friend." When I'd come to her with a problem, she'd ask, "Are you coming to me as if I'm a mother, sister, or friend? Because I'm not your parent, and I might go straight to Daddy with what you're about to tell me."

Although at the time I thought she just wanted to be around me, I now realize she was trying to give me a rest from a home filled with growing tension.

Recently I heard Nosizwe say, "Bakari taught me how to show affection. He was the 'I love you' kind of kid. Let me lay my head under you. We are very close. We were not huggers in our home. I do not hug my mom to this day, but Bakari taught us a different way. How could you not respond to a child who hugs you and tells you 'I love you'?"

• •

When I was a teenager, I tried my hand at picking melons. You could make $250 a week picking cantaloupe and $350 picking watermelons. You'd wait on the side of the road for farmers to pick you up in their trucks and take you to various farms. All day long you'd get in a line and pick up melons, or rather throw them. Good money, but the work was hard. Needless to say, for me, it got old fast.

Even though Denmark was black, there were still a few white establishments. And my father, in his day, couldn't eat at those white diners, and he couldn't try on clothes in the white stores. And yet, he grew up solidly middle class in Denmark, participated in Boy Scouts, read comics, and was an acolyte at St. Philips Episcopal Church on the campus of Voorhees College. He also attended middle and high schools on the college campus, too. When he was a boy, he asked his parents if he could try his hand at picking cotton. They agreed, though they whispered to one another that he wouldn't like it. And just like my watermelon picking, he didn't last long—two days.

· ·

In the Bible Belt, church was foremost, but we weren't those people who went to church on Monday, Wednesday, Saturday, and Sunday. Neither were we the "Easter families," the ones who go to church all dressed up once a year. We went to church every Sunday. When my grandparents were alive, I dreaded going to church with them because that meant we had to attend two churches—Bethel AME and Rome Baptist Church—because my grandparents, weirdly enough, and I still don't know why, attended two churches. When we moved to Denmark permanently in 1990, we became members of St. Philips. The mayor went there, as did the president of Voorhees College and some of the teachers in town.

Like my father before me, I was an acolyte (equivalent to an altar boy) from the time I was six. I lit candles, carried the cross, and assisted the pastor in anything he did. During communion, we served real wine. When no one was paying attention, the acolytes would finish off the leftover wine—and top it with a swish of used holy water.

Although we weren't the most religious family on the street, my parents were very prayerful. We always said grace before every meal; even now I say grace. I may not say it out loud, but I always close my eyes and bow my head, no matter who I'm with.

• •

The Sellers name conjured up pluck and honor, and also some pain in Denmark. Using *Game of Thrones* as a reference, we were the Starks of Winterfell. Pop often got a smackdown for being around the Sellers. "You think you better 'cause you with the Sellers," people would say to him. But Pop was no fool. When he got in trouble, he'd quickly use the Sellers name like a charm.

My father returned to Denmark because he believed he needed to complete what his parents had set out to do—to uplift a community that had sunk into poverty. My grandfather, Cleveland Sellers Sr., was a respected businessman in Denmark. Everyone knew him because you either ate fish sandwiches at his cafes or he drove you around in his cab. You even might have patronized his juke joint, or if you were visiting the local colleges, you stayed in his motel. A World War II veteran, he had twenty rental properties and a six-room motel, which now sits empty by the old family home. My brother recalls playing in my grandfather's office, watching him loan people a little money, more than a bank would give them, but knowing also how to get his money back. When people needed something done—maybe a son was in jail or someone owed money they couldn't afford—they'd call my grandfather.

My grandmother came from Upstate, in Abbeville. She was a product of two loving parents—a white father, who couldn't live with his black family, and a black mother. She became a dietitian at what's now known as Denmark Technical College. She worked with the homeless and was a board member of the NAACP. When my father realized that a boy in his school was eating food from the garbage, my father told his mother, who began making her son an extra sandwich each day to give to the boy.

When my father was ten years old, he heard about the killing of a fourteen-year-old boy named Emmett Till. The Chicago boy was visiting his grandfather in Money, Mississippi, in 1955 when he was murdered for allegedly whistling at a young white woman. Mamie Till, Emmett's mother, insisted on having an open casket at his funeral, leading to the picture of her son's mutilated face being published in *Jet* magazine and other media. A mainstay in every black home, *Jet* lined living room tables or was tucked neatly on bathroom shelves. It included celebrity stories, crime briefs, and a little gossip. *Jet* seeped into the collective psyche of black folk and figured out exactly what we wanted to read. There were also pictures of black beauties in swimsuits, which boys like me rushed to see every week.

When *Jet* published the picture of Till in his open casket, black kids all over carried the magazine to school. My father's

African-American teachers didn't shy away from telling the students the truth, even though the textbooks my father used described black people as lazy and even set forth rules about how blacks should be handled. Till's death, the teachers explained, meant black boys and girls had a job to do—to end injustice against our people.

Till's death took hold of my father, so much so that at age sixteen he was inspired to organize a sit-in demonstration at a local white restaurant in Denmark. All over the United States, little brown boys and girls with names like Stokely, Jesse, Kathleen, Angela, and Cleveland were reading *Jet*, and they came together years later in massive demonstrations during the 1960s. My father's inability to forget the face of a murdered black boy is also what motivates me to this day and what got my father in so much trouble in the first place.

You see, in Denmark, people knew my last name for something else too.

That's where my story begins.

I

The Wounds Have Not Healed

"Don't Be a Dead Hero"

February 8, 1968, is one of the most important days of my life—even though it was sixteen years before I was born.

That day about two hundred black students at South Carolina State College attempted to desegregate an all-white bowling alley in Orangeburg. After several days of protests, highway patrol officers lined up along an embankment and fired into the group of unarmed students. They killed three young black men, all age eighteen or younger—Samuel Hammond Jr., Delano Middleton, and Henry Smith—and shot and wounded twenty-eight others.

The tragedy took place in eight to ten seconds—the time it takes for two sips of coffee or to tie your shoes. It's the amount of time a bull rider must remain on a bull to score. Sociologists say it takes eight seconds to make an impression

19

on someone. And it took that amount of time to shatter so many lives.

In those few seconds, the sky lit up with gunfire, students fled for their lives as they were being pelted in the back, in the head, and in the soles of their feet with buckshot from shotguns hunters used to kill large game like deer. One youngster was shot in the face, knocking out sixteen teeth; bullets pierced another's heart; and yet another, a high school student waiting for his mother, a maid at the college, was hit six times.

The shooting stopped as fast as it started, but for some it never ended.

One of the people wounded that night was Cleveland Sellers, my father. A young, married civil rights activist at the time, my daddy was arrested, thrown in a jail cell, and was the only person to spend time in prison for instigating a riot that never happened.

My parents have always talked to me about the Orangeburg Massacre. I am pretty sure it was whispered to me when I was in my mother's belly.

I've also heard the story from the mouths of those wounded that night. I've heard it from the relatives of the dead, and of course I've heard it from the "agitator" himself. And with each hearing, I always discover something new.

I am a child of the civil rights movement. There's a photograph of me in the arms of "Uncle" Jesse Jackson, who was holding me while I fed a horse. I was the campaign baby during his second run for president in 1988. He was just one of my many "uncles" and "aunts," all of them legends and famous in their own right. I grew up answering the phone and then saying, "Dad, Uncle Julian [Bond] is on the phone," or "Uncle Stokely [Carmichael] wants you," or "It's Aunt Kathleen [Cleaver]."

And while those uncles and aunts have inspired my success, they also connected me to the past, providing me with a useful playbook for the years to come.

My sister was right. I was a strange child, a very old soul. My father was intentional with me, and I was receptive. He never stopped showing me the realities of life. Maybe my sense of purpose was developing sooner and faster than in most children. As a result, my early knowledge of the injustices of the civil rights era has left me with a heavy heart, even as a child, with so many tears but also with hope—and a mission. My father's path and my own are tangled together over the same bloody ground. My goal, like his, is to help heal this nation's divide.

My father, who always explained what happened that night with great deliberation and calm, was sure to mention every name involved in the Orangeburg Massacre because he didn't want us to grow up thinking that the only civil rights heroes were Rosa Parks and Martin Luther King Jr. Heroes, he wanted us to know, still walk among us.

The story he tells about the massacre often comes with great imagery, as he and I trek to South Carolina State where it all happened. He points to where the trash can was positioned that allowed him a few seconds after being shot in the left arm to get away from the police and to help another wounded student. Or he points to where the students stood on a little hill where the police fired shots at them.

In 1968, my father was only twenty-three, a year older than I was when I became a member of the South Carolina House of Representatives. Back then, he was a well-known leader of the Student Nonviolent Coordinating Committee (SNCC). Several years earlier, he had dropped out of Howard University in order to work with SNCC in Mississippi, where he searched for three missing activists.

My grandfather was against my father's activism because he could see the rising tension on television, and my father kept him updated in letters. In one letter my grandfather begged Daddy to come home. "The motel plan is waiting for you. Please come home, you have been away long enough. It's time for you to return to school. I can't sleep," he wrote. "I am always thinking about you. . . . If you want to fly home call me. I will make all arrangements. Please let me see you Thanksgiving. We are planning to see Gwen [his sister]. Please don't be a dead hero."

. .

My father had promised his mother he'd go back to college and get his degree. Orangeburg was the perfect place to fulfill that promise because it had two historically black colleges and was located only about twenty-five miles northeast of Denmark. The town of fourteen thousand people also had something else: a history of protest. The Orangeburg Massacre was part of a longer narrative. Student demonstrations were nothing new in that community.

My father's friend Martin Luther King Jr. had delivered speeches in Orangeburg—and presided over the small wedding ceremony of my father and his first wife in the famous basement of Ebenezer Baptist Church in Atlanta. The newlyweds rented a house in Orangeburg, and my father set about trying to teach African-American history and empowerment to its black residents.

That winter, students at South Carolina State had other ideas. They had their minds set on desegregating the local All-Star Bowling alley. My father, however, believed the time for sit-ins, marches, and demonstrations had passed. Instead, his goal in Orangeburg was to ignite an interest in the black power movement, black identity, and African history. Although not a student at State, he found an audience on campus. The members of the student chapter of the Black American Coordinating Committee knew my father was a veteran activist and that he had worked closely alongside Stokely Carmichael, his former roommate at Howard University, and Dr. King.

"We were not interested in the bowling alley until the students got beat up," he explains to me. "With three [consecutive] nights of gunfire, I recognized the tension had escalated. We tried to work with the administration and faculty to see if we could come up with strategies and help the students get out of the box they were in."

The violence started on Tuesday, the second day of the protest, when a student was arrested for cursing at a patrolman. Angry about the arrest, a large crowd of mostly students from South Carolina State, about three hundred in all, returned to the parking lot of the bowling alley. The mood was tense, but not violent until a fire truck showed up, infuriating the demonstrators, who remembered a thousand peaceful protesters being hosed several years earlier in Orangeburg.

When someone shattered the glass door of the bowling alley, "about fifty policemen rushed out, swinging wooden batons and just slamming them down on dozens of co-eds, who ended up with lacerations across their heads and beatings across their backs," my father remembers. "In some cases, police were on either end holding the girls by their arms while another officer came down across their backs with batons."

Why is this so important to me, and why should it be important to all of us? We have to recognize the inequity of authoritarianism and its violent remnants that remain today. People always question whether racism is involved when unarmed African Americans are shot by police. But do we really need researchers, such as those from Boston University in the *Journal of the National Medical Association* in 2018, to tell us that structural racism is definitely related to police shootings? The university's public health researchers said people are wrongfully assuming that individual cops are out to get black people; rather, the problem lies within "all of society" and how it has treated black people for centuries.

Back in the 1960s, my father knew what could happen to someone like him. "Accidents do happen," he always says. To give you an idea of my father's commitment to activism, all you have to do is walk through my childhood home. Casually tucked under books in my father's library is a picture of

Dad standing with Martin Luther King Jr. and one of him at the age of eighteen sitting in the Oval Office with President Lyndon Baines Johnson. There's another photograph of my father with Muhammad Ali, Stokely Carmichael, and Elijah Muhammad, and several photos with Dr. King or with Dad standing or sitting near Uncle Stokely or Uncle Julian.

In all the photographs, my father is slightly in the shadows of these more boisterous men, because he knew that the loudest become targets. Still, his work and image brought him great attention—especially from the FBI and the governor of South Carolina, who was hell bent on blaming everything that happened in Orangeburg on him. Days before the shooting, my father recognized the not-so-subtle signs that he alone had been chosen to be the scapegoat for the uproar.

For example, his simple little rental house across from South Carolina State stood out because a tank was targeting it from the middle of the street. "That tank barrel was pointed directly at my house. I knew I couldn't stay there," my father says. "That would have been the incident that they needed to get rid of the black advocate. They would have claimed there was an exchange of fire, and they had to use the tank, and they are so sorry that it happened. And I shouldn't have been there."

My father also recognized that the powers that be, particularly Governor Robert McNair and the FBI, were developing a narrative. They began to publicly say that "black power advocates" were responsible for riling up the students, that it wasn't just the white police officers and politicians. "There were not a lot of people who were standing up saying the police had done anything wrong," he tells me. "Rather, it was 'the police are our *friends*.' You even had black folk who were beginning to say that and beginning to take on a kind of anti–black power tone. They'd say, 'We don't want that,' and 'we want our students to learn,' and 'we don't want anyone out there protesting.'"

This is human nature. Few people will stand up for justice. Even today, too many well-meaning people of all races, genders, and ages are at a loss for how to fight back. Martin Luther King Jr. once said, "In the end, we will remember not the words of our enemies, but the silence of our friends."

Once Governor McNair started publicly saying that "outside black agitators" were stirring up the students, my father knew things were going to get very bad for him. "I was the only black advocate around campus at the time, and I had enough experience to know when something and someone is being set up," he says, reminding me that he had been in Selma, Alabama; had attended the 1963 March on Washington; and had spent a year in Mississippi from 1964 to 1965 where the activists Andrew Goodman, James Cheney, and Michael Schwerner were murdered. His job had been to go out and search for the three in the middle of the night.

He knew from those days that he had to decide who he could trust. In Mississippi, the mostly black farmers had served as the eyes and ears of civil rights workers. "The farmers would go out during the day, calling themselves hunters, but they would come back and tell us where an old barn was located, and where wells were, or ravines were where hostages could be held, bodies could be put," Daddy tells me. "We've seen some tough times. There were times when fear should have been the greatest, but what always stuck out in my mind was, how do we eliminate the situation? How do we get out of it with as many lives saved as possible?"

As the South Carolina governor and police continued with the rhetoric of blaming the "black power advocates" in Orangeburg, my dad knew the trap had been set. "I was almost certain that I wasn't going to be able to get out of it," he says, "but I was going to do my best to keep myself and the students from getting killed."

After three days of all-night meetings in Orangeburg, he needed sleep. When a student offered his dorm room, my father accepted. Shortly after dozing off, he heard a knock at the door. A student told him he heard gunfire and thought my father should know. A veteran activist, he was worried because one thing he knew was that demonstrations should never happen at night.

At this time in the story, my father points to the open hill where a group of male students once stood. "It was dark, but no gunfire, nothing. As I got closer, I could see men in white helmets down the hill. I could see they had weapons, rifles and shotguns. I looked across the street, and there at Lowman Hall I saw a group of male students."

They were standing in a circle trying to figure out what to do next, and seventy heavily armed law enforcement officers were watching them. The students were agitated, upset about what had happened to the female co-eds the day before. And then, my dad noticed Henry Smith, one of the men who was killed that night. "I wanted to tell him that police were right down the hill, and they were armed. It was night and you could hardly see. I wanted to tell Henry that we needed to move this group to the interior of the campus. That's what I wanted to tell him, but I never did. I did get to him. I might have said 'Henry.' That's when the darkness turned to light, when the police started shooting."

• •

The Orangeburg Massacre was the first deadly shootout to happen on a college campus involving police. It occurred two years before the well-known shooting at Kent State University, during which four white students were killed, and two months before the assassination of Martin Luther King Jr. But the tragedy barely permeated the nation's consciousness. What began as a racially inspired shooting swiftly turned into a multifarious cover-up by senior officials of the state of South Carolina. At first, the cover-up worked, but then it didn't.

On the night of the shootings, police described the massacre to reporters as a two-way shootout between black students and highway patrol officers. Police claimed they were defending themselves, though there would never be any evidence to prove that even one student on the campus possessed a weapon that evening. To validate their story, the officers sought to pin the calamity on one man: my father.

My father still believes the patrol officers were coming up the hill that night to find him. We later learned during the trials that they knew for certain he was within the crowd. Peo-

ple after the shooting in Orangeburg began to say they con-
fused Henry Smith, one of the three young men killed, for my
dad. And it wasn't just their afros; my father and Henry Smith
looked so similar that five decades later my father looks like an
older version of him.

"I think the police could see me going across the street under the lamp post because I had a large afro, and you could
see my silhouette on the bottom of the hill where the police
were. I think they knew this was the time to pull the plug on
the trap."

After the shooting, wounded students fled to the college
infirmary or carried others there. It was pure mayhem: the
room was packed with wounded students, scared and lying
bleeding on the floor. There was only one nurse and there
were no ambulances, though the campus was filled with all
types of law enforcement officers, who quickly became aware
of what had just happened. Teachers, coaches, and other students transported the wounded and dying from the infirmary
to the all-black unit of the hospital, but my father refused to go
with them, believing that if the police found him there, he'd
surely be killed. But the nurse told him that if he didn't get his
wounded arm tended to, he'd be dead anyway.

At the hospital, my father noticed a black security guard
he had seen on campus. They locked eyes. Minutes later, the
sheriff was charging toward my father, asking whether he was
Cleveland Sellers. My father was arrested at the hospital as he
waited to get his wounds looked at.

There is a famous black-and-white photograph of my father taken at about this time in his story, shortly after he had entered the all-black unit of the hospital. He is tall, slim, and handsome. His afro, skinny jeans, and Converse shoes give him a hip modern-day look. Interestingly enough, he looks more like a taller Childish Gambino, the rapper and actor, than a Martin Luther King Jr.

Dad is smiling in the picture, which belies the horror he found himself in. His stature and picture of unruffled cool makes him appear as if he were merely superimposed into a vintage photograph, totally detached from the wild-eyed white patrolmen surrounding him. The truth is, he was somewhere in between "unruffled" and "horror." The photograph is real, even though he had to pretend to himself, just for a moment, that none of that was happening to him.

"I know what happens to you when you get caught like Goodman, Schwerner, and Cheney got caught by the sheriff's deputies and eventually ended up dead," he says. "So, I called out to the many students who were in the hospital: 'I am with the sheriff. If anything happens to me, I want you all to re-member I am with the sheriff.' Then I said it again: 'I'm with the sheriff.'"

But instead of taking my father on a long deadly drive, the officers took him to court where he was charged with arson, inciting a riot, battery with intent to kill, property damage, breaking and entering, and grand larceny. The charges—indeed, the entire situation—were so absurd, my father ex-plains, all he could do was laugh when he was taken out of the courtroom before a gaggle of reporters and photographers.

That's when the photograph was taken. "The lies. It was like a fantasy," he says now. "I smiled because what else could I do? I sure wasn't going to cry."

When the Torch Has Been Passed

In 2014, Julian Bond, one of my legendary "uncles," requested to interview me for the Explorations in Black Leadership video collection. He asked me to reflect on the legacy of the Orangeburg Massacre. I was a young state representative and tried my best to answer in the most straightforward way I knew how.

At the time, Uncle Julian was professor of history at the University of Virginia. Many influential people had been interviewed, from the New York politician Charles Rangel to Supreme Court justice Clarence Thomas. The interview would be the last time I talked to Uncle Julian, because he died in 2015 of an aneurism. His death hit my father hard. They were contemporaries and true friends for fifty years.

During that interview Julian and I discussed how hard it is to believe that one of the most vicious incidents in the civil rights era happens to be one of the least known. "Everyone knows about Kent State," I said, "and I truly believe that if the lessons had been learned from Orangeburg, then we could have saved a number of lives at Kent State."

Julian wanted to know my feelings about the student protesters at South Carolina State who disagreed with my father and, come hell or high water, wanted to shut down any semblance of segregation, even at a bowling alley. "I think of that gumption or that courage, that audacity, for them to believe they could break down the last barrier of segregation in South Carolina," I said, "it just showed the strength of that generation, that young generation."

The protesters in Orangeburg, I believe, did not protest in vain. Governor McNair's 2007 obituary in the *New York Times* says that his insistence that "black power" influences had fueled the unrest severely hurt his standing in the black community and foiled any chances he had to join Vice President Hubert Humphrey's bid for the Democratic presidential nomination in 1968.

That day with Julian, I discussed my thoughts about how the deaths of the three young men during the Orangeburg Massacre created a chip on my shoulder—one I carried as I went about my legislative duties. As a political servant, I explained, I try to do things that I feel will help continue their mission, even though the goals might have changed.

Although my father's generation, the Emmett Till generation, speaks through us and lives among us, I believe we still have to carry their torch. There are so many parallels. Just as my father lived for Emmett Till, my task is to live for the people who have died at the hands of the law in my generation—Michael Brown, Terence Crutcher, Sandra Bland, and so many more. I see them all as martyrs. Their alleged crimes were not death penalty crimes, but still they died. Similar to Emmett Till, these victims were not given the benefit of their humanity; instead, they were treated as something less than human.

It all became crystal clear to me when I heard and saw what happened to Michael Brown in Ferguson, Missouri, in 2014. After his death, we now know that the words "hands up and don't shoot" don't protect anyone. Although there really was a tussle, that doesn't matter. Brown did not have a gun, and he should not have been killed. The image of Brown lying dead under a sheet for hours upon hours in the sweltering sun, while in the distance you can hear the aching bellows of his mother, made me realize that in Ferguson, they didn't care about Michael Brown, they didn't care that he was a human being, and they certainly didn't care that he was a black man.

Born to Do This

I can recall with great clarity the day my father's story was burnished in my psyche. I was in third grade and got called to the principal's office. My father was picking me up to attend the twenty-fourth annual memorial service of the Orangeburg Massacre. There's a picture of him at the service with his hands wrapped around me. The president of South Carolina State University is standing right beside us. I'm wearing my school uniform and a blue jacket. My father is wearing a long coat. I recall his grip. That's when it dawned on me that the moment was larger than myself.

Every year I returned to another anniversary ceremony at South Carolina State University to hear the memories of those wounded students. When I was a child, I was always ready to go wherever my dad went. "Bakari loved riding with me," he often recalls. "So, when I was ready to go, he'd get his coat."

My mother says that besides looking exactly alike, my father and I share a similar temperament. She says, "They are sensitive, not soft. They are both easy to cry to this day." She respects how deeply I feel about the Orangeburg Massacre but wonders whether it has taken too much out of me.

I think this is a fair assessment. Like I've said many times, I'm angrier about what happened back then than my own father is today.

Why did my father pick me to teach these lessons to? I believe he saw something in me. I could be a serious child, and he recognized I was responsive to what he was showing me. Deep down, was he preparing me to pass the torch to? I think he'd agree that he was.

During the many memorials we have attended together, I talked to the family members of people killed and to those wounded back in 1968. I heard their stories and learned to recognize when they were revealing emotional scars. My father to this day tells people, "When Bakari was a little boy, he'd ask everyone a hundred questions."

I realize now my father was doing more than just allowing me to see history up close. He was helping me to learn the importance of empathy as a balm against suffering.

I learned that Delano Middleton, the youngest of the three young men killed that day, was a high school student whose mother worked as a maid at the college. He asked her from his hospital bed to read Psalm 23 to him. Then, after repeating it himself, he died. I also heard from people who still live with the bullets inside of them, and those who still live with nightmares.

Some might say the things I heard were too horrid for a child to know, but my father thought it was important, just like he thought it was important for me to join him during his visits with prison inmates and conversations with gang members.

In retrospect, maybe I asked "a hundred questions" of the survivors of the massacre because I needed to understand their scars to better understand ours. The injustices that occurred that night left mothers without their sons. It left the pages of my beloved state's history stained in blood, and it left my sister to be born when her father was in prison. My sister's middle name is Abidemi, which means "born while father is away." I believe it's one of my father's biggest regrets that she met him for the first time in a room in the Columbia Correctional Institute.

From the time my father was arrested until he was pardoned in 1990, he was like a leper, and we were like refugees. My father's loving parents worried about him, warning him not to return to South Carolina, which is why me and my siblings were born in North Carolina rather than in Denmark, where he was born and where I was later raised. Before the pardon, my father struggled with getting jobs and endured visits from the FBI at the jobs he was able to get.

Despite that pardon and the fact that books have been written clearing my father's name, some people in South Carolina still put the blood and tragedy on his shoulders.

There is another thing that still haunts us: the eerie re-semblance between Henry Smith, who died on February 8, and my father, and the widely believed theory that police may have murdered the wrong man. By no means were we the only ones who struggled after the tragedy. Indeed, it took my father many years to convince some of the wounded students to tell their stories. Some are still suffering from emotional stress. They will never return to Orangeburg or the campus. They can't even look toward the direction of the campus when they drive on I-26.

My father's wounds have never healed completely—the lin-gering blame, the memory of bloodshed, the fact that still so few people know about the massacre. And there's never been any reconciliation with any of the victims' families. While still a member of the South Carolina House of Representatives, I unsuccessfully called for a state-convened blue-ribbon panel in 2009 to launch a formal investigation. The fact that the government still refuses to further investigate the tragedy angers many African Americans, especially my father, but for others it's a relief.

There are folks in South Carolina who believe the students were merely unmatched. That would suggest there was a bat-tle, but there's no battle in a slaughter. The students were un-armed, shot in the back. In South Carolina, people say you "slaughter" a chicken or pig, but they never say you do battle with them. Several investigative journalists dubbed the trag-edy a "massacre," but in Orangeburg, especially among white people, what to call this event has always been controversial.

A year after the tragedy, nine patrolmen were put on trial, but a jury took only two hours to clear their names. Two and a half years after the massacre, my father was convicted of a riot that was never part of the original investigation. In 1973, he spent seven months in prison. However, important information was unearthed during the trials. On the day of the massacre, 450 members of the National Guard and 127 patrolmen were in town, many of them on the college campus. What my father suspected was also true: federal agents and the police knew of him, they knew of his affiliation with the SNCC and his friendship and work with Stokely Carmichael. They also wanted to believe my father was the cause of everything that happened in Orangeburg, but they could show no evidence to prove that.

Today, some white folks near and around Orangeburg agree that something horrible happened—but it happened long ago. They say that continuing to bring it up all the time is just stirring up a hornet's nest. They often point out that the students weren't angels. Because of original misinformation, some people to this day still believe that a black student shot first in the direction of law enforcement officers that night, even though there's never been any evidence that that ever happened.

• •

A week before the special ceremony in 2018 honoring the fiftieth anniversary of the Orangeburg Massacre, Bill Hine, a white history professor at South Carolina State and a family friend, asked me to give the keynote speech. First Lady Michelle Obama and President Barack Obama had been asked to do so, as well as Senator Cory Booker and former Massachusetts governor Deval Patrick, but none of them was able to do it. I threw every name I could think of at Hine, because I knew it would be too draining for me. But in the end, I agreed and decided to talk about the wounds from the tragedy that have never healed—including my own.

I paced back and forth before giving the speech. If I could get through the first part, I'd make it through the entire speech before breaking down.

I walked to the microphone and began to speak. "I saw the scars and heard the story again and again," I told the crowd. And as much as I tried to stop them, the tears flowed. The sorrow I felt was physical, like someone had ripped out my heart. I couldn't stop the tears. "Shit," I said, before taking a breath. "It's physically painful to think about that night so ripe with potential and possibility erupting into violence and tragedy and loss, and I wasn't even there. Still it hurts like nothing else I know—in my chest, behind my eyes, and all over my body—a living pain of a cultural memory and a realization that I live in a state where something like this could have happened. And they tell us to let it go. 'Don't tell that story again. We don't want to hear it. Don't go back to that place . . . don't say their names.' But we have to, not because we want to remember . . . but because we can't forget."

I said I took pride knowing that if the tragedy happened today, not only would those officers have to answer for their actions, but they'd have to answer to someone who looked like me.

And so, it remains the most important day of my life. My father's path and my own are woven together over the same bloody ground.

Dad made his mark on history that night in 1968 and stayed on the path with other leaders, from Martin Luther King Jr. to John Lewis to uncles Stokely and Jesse. He and my mother Gwen raised their three children to stand up and speak for social justice. As a lawyer, politician, and civil rights activist, I see my life as an extension of my father's journey. In this new era of civil rights, in which politicized young activists have a direct impact on the nation's laws and policies, I am a bridge between his work and the achievement of our common goal of racial equity.

And yet, fifty years after Cleveland Sellers, my father—a professor, college president, and civil rights activist—was on the front lines of the civil rights struggle, I find myself in a country that looks too much the same. In my time, in *our* time, some of the most racist remarks come from the very top, where the president himself panders to the worst in us to score points with a particular political demographic.

II

Black and Forgotten

When I say that Denmark is part of the forgotten South, I mean that the simple dignities we all expect as humans, such as clean water, a community hospital, and more than one grocery store, are ignored. This is a town where it's not unusual to spot someone driving their lawnmower, the one they use to cut white residents' lawns, to the Piggly Wiggly, the only major grocery store in town. It's also not unusual to see adults, even the elderly, riding bikes—often children's bikes—but not for exercise. Instead, they can't afford a car—the taxes, the gas, the insurance, and the maintenance are all too much.

Riding a bike can be tough if you're isolated in rural South Carolina. If the tropical heat doesn't get to you in the summer, our "no-see-um" gnats will. Imagine riding an old bicycle while clutching a bag or two of groceries in one hand, swatting invisible bugs with the other, and trying to balance the jig-gling cycle, sometimes on dirt roads.

My mother says Denmark's poverty is akin to what you might observe in a developing country. The bike riding, she believes, is a form of resilience—"making do."

· ·

It's easy to be blind to the endurance of, or to completely ig-nore, the people whom others may think of as "backwoods," hidden from the rest of the world. However, I see us as less "backwoods" and more "dirt road." If you're from rural South Carolina, you've ridden down a dirt road to get home. You'll understand the difficulty of cleaning a pickup truck after you've driven down a muddy path. And if it's raining, you know how to maneuver the holes.

Dirt road living is who we are, allowing us to understand early on that life can be slippery, but we figure out how to nav-igate the unpredictable paths—paths that can go from gentle to muddy and treacherous in minutes. Those dusty roads have been leading us and connecting us from one place to another for generations. After the Great Migration, when five to six million black folk left the South and moved north and west to cities such as Chicago, Philadelphia, and New York, those who left called the ones who remained "country bamas."

Those same black folk who look down on us for staying have grandmothers and great-grandfathers who were reared on these same dirt roads. Maybe most importantly, every ounce of black cultural liberation, every bit of political ideology, first derived from the South. The spirit by which we have fought to gain those not-so-tangible ideals, such as freedom and justice, have all emerged from us country folk—and we'll accept that.

If you are black and country, you inherit a rich cultural legacy, one born out of that Black Belt soil that rises from the coast of Charleston, with all the rotten smells of pluff mud emitting from the marshlands and the taste of stone-ground grits stored in our memories.

When you grow up in these left-behind communities where schools are falling apart and hospital doors are slammed shut, the only real thing that your families can give you is a sense of self and the notion of being unapologetically black. That pride allows some of us to maneuver out of the dirt roads to Wall Street. But our families also pass down something else—poverty.

228 Years of Catching Up

There's enough research out there to show that people born into poverty often become an heir to it, which means poverty is passed down from one generation to another. African Americans are less likely to rise from this intergenerational transmission of poverty compared with other groups. There are many reasons for this, including unusually high incarceration rates, education inequalities, drugs, segregation, workplace discrimination, and lack of male role models.

For example, when my friend Pop was a little boy, he looked

at his surroundings and the people therein and decided he wanted something different, but how could he break the cycle? Three years before I met Pop, he'd endured a heavy loss. His father was killed in a car crash, right behind Voorhees College. He was driving drunk and hit a large oak tree.

The car was totaled, and as Pop would say decades later in his heavy southern twang, "He busted his brains out." Pop, who was nine when it happened, went to the scene because "I had to see it for myself."

It was Christmastime and all Pop had wanted that year was a computer. As he stared into the twisted metal that was once his father's green Plymouth, Pop could see the remains of an Apple computer inside the car. From that moment on, Pop developed a severe distaste for computers. "I type only with two fingers," he says. "I had no interest to learn to do it right."

His mother, who worked odd jobs, running nightclubs and working at restaurants, tried her best to raise six children by herself.

There's a question I'm often asked. It's a question I dislike, and I am sure many African Americans also dislike it, because the very heart of the question dismisses so much important history. The query usually goes like this: "You know, all of these immigrant groups come to this country and thrive. Why haven't African Americans been able to break through?"

The question discounts hundreds of years of slavery, and then years of degradation brought upon us by the oppression of Jim Crow. It dismisses generations of white advantage and pretends we all came here and remain here on the same level, as if white privilege is based on merit. For instance, many European immigrants, who arrived long after African Americans, acquired government land for nearly free in order to accelerate the settlement of the West. They were given every opportunity to have their material needs met. Black people, on the other hand, built a nation and broke free from bondage, and yet legal segregation in Denmark ended only in 1972.

The question dismisses how the nation's lengthy past of racial inequality has added to an enormous gulf in accumulated fortunes, and with it a disproportionate gap of opportunity: If economic trends continue, black families in the United States will have to wait two centuries to accumulate the same amount of wealth white Americans enjoy today. The average household wealth of white families has grown 85 percent, to $656,000, in the past thirty years, according to the Corporation for Enterprise Development and the Institute for Policy Studies, while that of blacks has risen only 27 percent, to $85,000. White families have almost ten times the net worth of black families. Educated white Americans make three times more than their equally educated black counterparts. Now think about Denmark, where nearly everyone is struggling to survive. If the estimates are true, it will take much longer than two centuries for us to catch up.

• •

What a person like Pop survived in Denmark is being forgotten. The media equate rural America to white America; and that's not only an untrue portrait, but it influences how the public perceives the nation's crossroads. People of color make up one-fifth of rural America, and their poverty and high school dropout rates are much higher than those of white rural Americans. Half of Denmark's residents live below the poverty line; and most of the children in Denmark's schools are on the free lunch program, which is a true measure of just how poor a rural community is. The railroads and corporations that used to provide jobs during my father's day are all gone, which is why many young, fatherless men like Pop found themselves selling drugs—crack cocaine and Molly (which in other places is called Ecstasy).

After Pop's father's death, the boy put all his attention on two things: football and soccer. If you ask my family how we met Pop, most of us will have a different story; however, there's a consistent narrative thread. After moving to Denmark, my father took over the city's recreational center, which his mother had previously run. My daddy wanted to add a soccer component to the summer program. A teacher told him about a boy named Jamil, whom everyone called Pop. The adults believed Pop would benefit from keeping busy at the recreational center, and Pop wanted that, too.

In Denmark, we don't have gangs, but we have families you don't mess with, and we have neighborhoods. Pop's neighborhood is called "the Hookz." I lived on one side of the tracks, in the Sato community, and he lived on the other, which could be why Pop and I see Denmark very differently. I see just one Denmark—desolate, sometimes bleak, but at the same time safe, peaceful, and heartbreakingly beautiful. We were all struggling, but he saw one side of the struggle and two Denmarks: the good side and the "bad side."

That's why, he says, he decided to unofficially come stay with us, "to get away from the bad side." In the tough section of town, as he puts it, "you always see fellas sitting around drinking, smoking weed, selling drugs, toting pistols, or they want to fight. On Bakari's side you didn't have none of that, it was really quiet, and everybody stayed to themselves."

Pop saw no beauty—just boys downtown drinking gin and rolling dice. He would say, "there's a lot of unsolved crimes," meaning the crimes are unsolved because those who commit them are often from somewhere other than Denmark, where everyone knows everyone else.

He is right about one thing. Although there were times we struggled financially, my family was not poor. My mother, who was a television anchor at a small station when we lived in Greensboro, began teaching business communication at South Carolina State, which was only twenty-five miles away from Denmark. I ended up going to primary school on the campus, the same campus where the Orangeburg Massacre happened. My father's opportunities were limited because of his prison record, but after he was pardoned, the world opened up to him, too. Jarrod Loadholt, my college roommate, who grew up in Orangeburg, often said, "Back home, children grew up reading about Cleveland Sellers in the history books. He's our Martin Luther King Jr."

I don't believe Pop knew anything about my father's infamous history when they first met in 1990. As the story goes,

Pop was hungry one day at the recreation center. He asked my sister, who was home from college for the summer and acting as an unofficial counselor, if he could get something to eat. Either he didn't like what the center was having for lunch that day or had missed lunch, but my sister, who Pop called "my girlfriend," walked him to our house and gave him a peanut butter sandwich and soup. If you ask everyone in my family how old Pop was at the time, they'd say he was my age, but he was actually twelve—double my age.

"Pop was just this cute little boy, like Bakari. I saw them as babies," my sister says.

In her mind, Pop was just six years old, like me; though probably it was more like I acted like I was twelve years old, like him. An old man in a six-year-old boy's body, I was still a sheltered child in a new town. I immediately took to Pop as we played video games and watched sports on television. I asked my parents to allow Pop to play with me from then on and encouraged them to drive us to his home to ask his mother if that was okay.

My father saw Pop as a good comrade for me, but he also believed he could be a father figure to the boy. After that first visit, Pop was always at our home. "I came and never left," he jokes. My mother, who could be described as uppity (or "bougie" if you're African American), didn't know what to think of Pop, who was a little rough around the edges. Eventually, he became her "fourth child" and another brother who joined me and my father as we traveled to Lumumba's basketball games or visited him at Morehouse College.

During one Easter Sunday church service, fifteen-year-old Pop was officially accepted as my parents' godchild. From then on, Pop called my father "Dad" and me "Bruh." And like most parents, my mother and dad were always having long talks with him about "messing up." My mother, not the person to hold back, "gave him shit," Pop often jokes.

If you ask Pop about messing up, he'll say, "I was always in trouble. I used to fight a lot. I got charged with selling drugs. Then later on in life I got charged with a lewd act—a girl lied about her age. We never had intercourse, but it messed up my life."

My father, in particular, was often trying to make sure Pop stayed out of trouble. Once, Pop took a knife to high school to prevent a fight from breaking out on the school bus. He was arrested, and Pop told the authorities to get ahold of Mr. Sellers. My father begged, cried, and pleaded with the authorities to not kick him out of school or send him to jail. Pop was expelled, but he didn't go to prison.

Can He Survive This?

The night Pop got shot in 2008, I was at a club watching the NCAA championship in Columbia. I received a text saying he was being airlifted to Richland Memorial Hospital, and since I was nearby, I went there immediately. I called my sister, who was a doctor-in-training at Richland, so she'd be waiting for him. I should have been worried, but I wasn't because Pop is one of the most resilient people I know. Somehow, he has always managed to survive. Several years before being shot, he'd been stabbed; he'd also been arrested for selling drugs and spent more than a year in prison. In an isolated town with no job prospects, Pop's life was typical.

He was playing cards on the night he got shot. Everyone was outside, drinking and having a good time. Pop saw a young man he knew hitting a woman, and so he told him to stop. He was always doing stuff like that because he saw himself as a protector. The young man left but returned with a gun.

Pop paid him no mind, even when the young man shot in the air and told Pop that if he walked toward him, he would shoot. Pop, always the person who wanted to stand up for the underdog, told the young man to put down the gun and approached him. The bullet clipped a piece of Pop's lung and came out in his right armpit. He was rushed to Bamberg County Hospital, which at the time was still Denmark's functioning local hospital, and then was airlifted to Richland in Columbia. He woke up screaming, proclaiming he was going to beat down the man who shot him, which prompted the physicians to give him morphine.

When his mother saw all the blood, she collapsed. Pop woke up and spotted his mother in a wheelchair, and then he lost it again, yelling and screaming. After that, he was either on life support or in a morphine-infused daze.

After we realized Pop would pull through, we felt a sting of anger. This might seem like a strange reaction, but seeing Pop's mother in so much torment frustrated my father and my mother to no end. My parents had driven her to the hospital;

we all observed her heartbreak. Pop had put himself at death's door again, and that was a lot to bear. Being a doctor, my sister had seen everything, including the nasty, bloody, behind-the-scenes events. "I was so pissed at Pop," she recalled years later, though I think she was more afraid we'd lose our "brother" and how that would crush all of us.

I don't remember feeling fearful, and my father doesn't remember going to Pop's room, but my sister recalls we were both visibly upset. That night after everyone had left the room, my six-foot-two-inch sister looked down on the sleeping Pop and said, "If you ever have my brother and my daddy crying at your bedside again for some foolishness, it's going to be you and me. If you went to hell or heaven, I'm still going to get you."

Pop doesn't doubt my sister made that promise. He admired her spunk, brilliance, and beauty ever since he was a hungry boy at the recreation center. He even named one of his daughters after her. He knows our anger was linked to the love we all felt for him.

In 2012, Bamberg Hospital closed its doors because of petty politics and lack of funds. The closing was a confluence of idiocy and stubbornness. It should have remained open. If Pop had been shot any time after that, he could have died. Who knows whether he could have survived the twenty-five-mile trip by ambulance to the next-closest hospital in Orangeburg? I hate to even imagine how many people may have lost their lives because there's no hospital in town anymore. As Pop says, "It could have been lights out" for him.

For a while after the shooting, Pop kept his distance from us, though he thought we were doing the same. He said that he wanted to prove to himself and to us that he could get his life in order. When I ran for South Carolina lieutenant governor in 2014, Pop called me and was on the streets holding up banners. Meekly, he told me and my father at different times that he wanted to go to college. "Mr. Sellers encouraged me to never give up even though I made some bad decisions," he says. "Bakari also encouraged me. Once they saw me take the initial steps, they supported me, and that meant a lot to me."

In 2013, Pop got his GED. Several years later, he earned an associate's degree in science at Denmark Tech. "I'm no dummy," he likes to say. In 2017, he got his bachelor's degree in business administration from Voorhees, with a focus in finance. He studied hard and graduated with distinction. He was inducted into the Alpha Kappa Mu Honor Society. Then, he spent one semester working on his master's degree at Claflin University in Orangeburg. By then, he had two children. His mother said he needed to get a job to support his family, so he quit graduate school. But what kind of job can a man with a prison record and no driver's license get in a town where there are no jobs? After all that studying and a college degree with honors, Pop, who's now forty, works for a company that makes kitchen sinks and doors and is paid eight dollars an hour.

Pop has no shame discussing his faults. He's the first to say he drank way too much, but he has cut down, now only drinking Busch Light. When he does get drunk, his heavy southern accent turns to a deep-throated mumble, which can make it hard to understand what he's saying if you don't know him, but I know him. He's never nasty or belligerent, only philosophical.

One recent winter night, Pop's voice on the telephone was crisp and clear. In the background, I could hear him talking to someone. It was my father, who had taken sandwiches and sodas to Pop's family. After my father pulled away in his truck, Pop wanted to know two things from me. The first was this: "If I'm Bakari's brother, why wasn't I invited to be in your wedding?"

The answer to the wedding question is simple: only two people were at my wedding—my stepdaughter and my brother Lumumba, who's now a minister. But I don't think that's really what Pop was asking me. I believe Pop was wondering whether his past scared me away. I needed to honestly consider my own possible failings in this regard. We were not around each other as much as when we were children, but I was always there for him. What should someone who has gained a certain amount of privilege do about a friend who hasn't? It's a very difficult question, and something many of us with siblings, parents, cousins, and old friends either struggle with or ignore.

My answer might not put me in a good light, but it's honest. The last thing I will do is talk down to someone like Pop, a grown black man who's made mistakes but has done his damnedest to turn things around. However, we all need moments of introspection. I will never push away Pop; he is as much a part of my life as he is part of the fabric of Denmark. But Pop needed the time he took to put his life together, to complete important things, like graduate from college. I think Pop realized there was a point where he had to grow up. It might sound harsh, but it's true. So many people had poured so much into him that Pop began to understand it was time to make a return on that investment. He began to change, I believe, when he had children.

Pop's second question was even deeper than the first. "The Sellers say they love me; then why did they leave me in the hood?"

For me, this is a frustrating question, and I call it bullshit. I will do anything for Pop, and I will never leave people behind. And for most of my adult life I've been a legislator—a representative elected to serve all the people in my district. My personal focus is on Pop, of course, but in my profession, I also focus on all the similar stories in Denmark, all the voices that go unheard that Pop represents.

For instance, in November 2018, I filed a lawsuit against the town of Denmark for unsafe water. Residents in my hometown had been complaining for ten years about the rusty-colored liquid that dripped from their faucets. Some collected water samples, and many drank only bottled water, despite the mayor saying everything was all right.

As I stood in a community meeting talking to those residents, all I could think of was how the world has forgotten Denmark. It wasn't until after a year-long investigation by CNN that we learned the state government for a decade had been adding a substance called HaloSan to one of the city's wells in order to regulate naturally occurring bacteria. Between my lawsuit and the national attention that Denmark finally received, I believe the water problem will one day be fixed. But nobody knows the long-term effects it might have on an entire generation. Will there be learning disabilities in a community that already has a ton of preexisting health issues, such as cardiovascular disease and diabetes? Will we ever know how this could have happened for ten years without anyone informing Denmark residents or without the permission of the federal government?

The indignity that people in my hometown suffer makes me feel physically ill, and I just have to do all I can to help. Sometimes, and in Pop's case, painfully, it's never going to be enough. When I think about Pop's question, I also have to think about his pain, and where he is coming from. As a child he wanted nothing more than to get away from trouble. He deeply loved his mother and siblings but enjoyed the order in our home and the quiet of our struggling neighborhood. We treated him as one of us. He ate, played, and slept beside us. Maybe deep down he wonders, How did the Sellers children become so successful and I haven't? I lived in that same house. Why am I not where they are now? I've made big changes in my life, but why am I not doing better?

He believes his prison record will haunt him for the rest of his life, despite his academic success and all the changes he made in his life. As far as the lewd act, he didn't have sex with the girl, but he still doesn't get a pass on that, even if she did lie about her age. He spent thirteen months in prison on a five-year sentence.

Pop says he has learned from all of his mistakes. And for that reason, and all his academic achievement, I view him as being successful—with still a ways to go. Yet even with all his accomplishments, and all the help he's received, there are things Pop won't achieve because he is shackled by his past, by poverty, and by the dirt roads of Denmark. I know people say we all must pull ourselves up by our bootstraps, but that doesn't give value to being poor, black, and isolated in America.

Before There Were Trolls, There Was Jiving

In rural, segregated areas like Denmark and Orangeburg, black people live similarly to how they lived during the Jim Crow era. Regardless of class, we reside in the same black neighborhoods, often attending the same black schools and the same black churches. The children play and grow up together among the same black families, regardless of who their parents are and how much money their parents make.

Segregation wasn't some remembrance of the past for us; it was, and is, our reality.

Pop, a child of a struggling mother, was my friend, but so was Jarrod, who was raised by two educators in nearby Orangeburg. His mother is an English teacher and has been teaching for almost fifty years in Orangeburg County. His father was a social worker with an advanced degree. But even though some of us had parents who were well educated, they were all from these rural outposts in South Carolina and very familiar with all the challenges of such communities.

"We grew up with guys who ran the gamut," Jarrod often says, "from those who ended up dead or selling drugs to those who ended up being doctors. They were all our friends."

I remember clearly the first time I met Jarrod, who would become my closest friend, my roommate throughout college, and one of my biggest supporters in life. But back on the first day of my sophomore year of high school, Jarrod was nothing less than petty. Since he was born and raised in Orangeburg, he grew up reading in middle school about the Orangeburg Massacre and my father, but none of that mattered on my first day at Orangeburg-Wilkinson High School.

I was a sophomore but new to the school. As I walked into my first class, there was Jarrod looking me up and down. To this day, he is more than happy to tell anyone who will listen about that moment. "I was one of the kids who would wait at the door to see what your new outfit looked like when you walked into the classroom. If what you were wearing was bad, we'd start jivin'."

Depending on where you're from, this game of monster putdowns is called playing "the Dozens" or rekking, signifying, ragging, but in rural South Carolina, we called it simply "jiving." The colossal one-liners that are the stars in this game of insults are "snaps." The best way to describe this game is verbal dueling, a tangle of raw offenses slung from one person to another until one of them gives up, or gets angry. Sometimes a bunch of people insult one person like in a Hollywood roast. Others go straight for the jugular, insulting "yo mama"; in fact, the "yo mama joke" is a subgroup of playing Dozens.

There have been sociological studies about the Dozens, a black American tradition that is believed to be linked to Africa or slavery, but no one really knows where it came from. What we do know is that it started in the rural, black South and spread to the streets of urban America long before rap.

That first day of class, I walked into a cloud of adolescent jabs targeted strictly at me and led by one person. Leaning against the door, Jarrod asked, "Who *is* this *kid*? No, please tell me he ain't wearing a family reunion T-shirt?"

"Ahhhh!" the rest of the boys shouted, and the jokes and laughter started immediately.

In between putdowns and pretending he could barely catch his breath, Jarrod asked, "Who the fuck is this kid?"

Some of the boys who had gone to school with me said that's so-and-so. But Jarrod didn't care who I was. He said, "Wait! This kid is wearing windbreaker pants, some sneakers that aren't new, and a family reunion shirt?"

The crowd of silly boys roared.

"He's tall, but probably 120 pounds soaking wet!"

Jarrod was on a roll.

"He has an afro. In fact, he looks just like a Q-tip!"

"Ahhhhhh!" the group roared.

After everyone settled down, Jarrod looked at me and said, "At the end of the day black folk like to look good, and in my opinion this kid looks terrible."

But here's what shocked them and what quickly got me in

the good graces of a group of boys who were all trying hard to be part of the "in" crowd: I laughed with them and as hard as they did. I was right there with them catching my breath and holding my stomach from all the laughter. My actions threw them off. The target of the snaps usually snaps back or gets upset or moves on, which is exactly the goal.

But why would I get angry? It was crystal clear to everyone, including me, that I hadn't done my due diligence, which was putting in the time and effort needed to look good for the first day of school, and that was a sort of sin. So, it would have been pure insanity to try to argue against the point with these kids, who had nearly perfected the art of jiving. Truth be told, Jarrod was right: I looked exactly like a Q-tip, skinny with an afro.

It didn't matter that the reason I didn't have a cool outfit was because I spent my ninth-grade year at a white school, where your first-day-of-school outfit wasn't a thing. I liked the teachers and the students at that school, but it was an hour each way from home, and I never got to see my friends. However, I started to quickly learn that I was even more out of place at this black high school.

The kids picked up that something was different about me, but they couldn't put their fingers on it. As it turns out, I entered high school at the age of twelve. When I was much younger, I had skipped two halves and a whole year. I went to kindergarten for a semester, and then after Christmas I was placed in first grade. I was also a good standardized test taker, resulting in my going to third grade the next year at Felton Laboratory School on the campus of South Carolina State. Yet as much as I might have been a mature little boy, a strange old man in a little boy's body, I could also be a socially awkward teen.

Here I was, this skinny kid with a big head, from the countriest dirt-road town. I was the perfect target during lunch, but I continued to laugh and learn. The truth? I had been teased for being the youngest since third grade, so there was nothing these boys could say that I hadn't already heard.

Orangeburg-Wilkinson had two thousand students, so lunch had to be in two different places: the main school and nearby Calhoun-Orangeburg Vocational Education Center. The truth is, lunch at the vocational center didn't help overcrowding. It was pure chaos. You had thirty minutes to either pay $1.25 for regular school food or buy a Chick-fil-A sandwich or a Papa John's slice of pizza, sit down, eat, snap, and laugh.

Our group consisted of Jarrod, Reggie Abraham, Tim Jennings, Ryan Brown, and Joseph Brandon. Reggie would start beatboxing, which is making hip-hop sounds with your mouth—like scatting but more percussive. Someone would often join with a rap. Depending on what day it was, we might start jiving. Someone would take a shot, and you had to shoot back. I'd say something like, "Jarrod's mama's so dumb, she takes an hour to cook Minute Rice."

He'd snap back, "Bakari's mama's so old, her memory's in black and white."

Then I'd say, "Yo' mama's so fat, when God said 'Let there be light,' he told her to move out the way."

Someone else would claim you got dressed in the dark, or that you're wearing your sister's hand-me-downs. None of it, of course, was true, and nothing was out of bounds.

We kept up the jokes in class, though we also remained earnest about our studies. One of our favorite teachers was Mrs. Miller, who taught AP history. She was serious, but she let us be ourselves—a group of AP kids who loved to tell jokes. Mrs. Miller allowed us to snap on each other as long as it wasn't out of bounds. Maybe she saw jiving as a true rite of passage. After all, most of the guys at the table did well in life. Reggie became a political operative and has worked for Stacey Abrams and Kamala Harris; after Jarrod finished a degree at Morehouse, he went on to Harvard; Ryan and Joseph are both doctors; and Tim, a cornerback, won the Super Bowl in 2007 with the Indianapolis Colts and later played for the Chicago Bears.

Not everyone at the table was as successful, but those who didn't have the opportunities that the rest of us had can still jive with the best of them and probably are wittier than any of us. To this day, those verbal acrobatics I learned back then still give me an edge, especially in the courtroom. Anything that someone says about me, I've already heard. It helps me to deal with social media trolls, to battle veteran politicians, and to be quick on my feet for television.

· ·

Mr. Brown, who taught philosophy, was a white teacher from New York City at this black high school in rural South Carolina. We had quite a few white teachers, but none from New

York. Jarrod and I did a lot of writing and loads of presentations in his class. We read books like *Zen and the Art of Motorcycle Maintenance*, which I remember as being heavy and challenging. Jarrod says no one forgets that book, but I don't know whether I read it for comprehension or to just get by.

Schoolwork came easily to me, but not through osmosis. Once I read something and wrote it down, I remembered it, digested it, understood it, and could spit it back. Part of the way I learned was natural, but some of it stemmed from the way my parents raised me and my siblings—always trying to challenge us, and introducing us to other adults, like my "uncles" and "aunts," who talked to us about grown-up issues.

My grandmother always said an idle mind is the devil's playground, meaning children shouldn't get too bored. My parents put us in situations that challenged us, which is likely why they didn't hesitate when my elementary teacher suggested I skip a grade. Now that I'm a parent, I can act on the belief that it's much better to challenge children than spend energy protecting them from failure.

My high school physics teacher realized the class wasn't difficult for me and let me leave to talk with one of my other favorite teachers, a young white woman who helped me figure out my future. My parents were encouraging me to go to a black undergraduate college, but I needed more direction. So I talked to the teacher about colleges I liked, what to study in college, and where I should go. She suggested books I should read, and we talked about books I'd already read.

Many people have stories about high school counselors undervaluing their abilities and not encouraging them to attend college. Although I was a straight-A student with very high SAT scores, I too was told to join the army rather than apply to Morehouse College. Such teachers and counselors don't mean to underrate students but to protect them from failing. When I was in high school, there were far too many cautionary tales of Orangeburg students not doing well at big colleges. In fact, all Jarrod and I heard was, "Don't be like Lenny." Lenny had graduated from Orangeburg-Wilkinson and went to Morehouse, but he failed and had to return home.

Teachers gave all they could, even when the state and government tied their hands; but the truth is that the schools didn't do a great job preparing rural children for a competitive twenty-first-century global curriculum. Across this country, tens of millions of students drop out of college before finishing a degree, and a large percentage of them are rural children, who may not be emotionally or academically ready for big institutions. So when teachers underestimated us, they just didn't want us to become cautionary tales.

But I knew I could finish college because I'd seen my sister and brother do it. I spent lots of time on the Morehouse campus with my brother Lumumba when I was around eleven and twelve. I was allowed to carry his and the other football players' helmets after the games. I had a front-row seat into college life and the intellectual conversations that were happening around us. I'd sit in my brother's bedroom listening and joining in on discussions on everything from charter schools to the socially conscious lyrics of southern hip-hop groups like

OutKast and Goodie Mob. My brother and his roommate would play a Goodie Mob jam, stop it, deconstruct what was just said, and start the song back up. We were strictly into southern rap. Atlanta hip hop, in particular, was big with us, and I'm sure that was part of the reason that going to school in that city appealed to me and Jarrod. In high school, Pastor Troy's "No Mo Play in GA" was huge. In college it was all OutKast and the Dungeon Family.

The moment my brother accepted Morehouse's offer, I saw an invisible network become visible. Graduates he didn't know were calling him. I was literally experiencing an element of the famous Morehouse mystique come alive.

Years later, I had no idea Jarrod got accepted at Morehouse until one of our counselors told him in church one Sunday that I was going to go there. Jarrod saw me in school and said, "Yo, you going to Morehouse?"

"Yeah, I'm going."

"Alright. I got my letter, let's be roommates."

"Cool," I said, and the rest, as they say, is history.

III

School Daze

The Making of a Morehouse Man

When I arrived at Morehouse College, I was only six-teen years old, but no one guessed my age because I was six-foot-five and some change. I arrived with Hercules, my four-foot-long ball python, which probably should have been a dead giveaway, but my age was a kept a secret, at least until my mother sent a huge bouquet of balloons to the dorm months later that said "Happy 17th Birthday." I was mortified, to say the least.

Although pets were prohibited on campus, Hercules lived in my dorm room without Michael, the residential director, ever finding out—maybe because Michael wasn't around much since he was newly married. Michael treated us like grown men, having only one rule: don't disrespect me and make me write you up.

Jarrod and I moved into Room 122 in the honors dorm called Graves Hall. It was one of those old-school college dorms with one twin bed to the right and another to the left. I had my snake, and Jarrod had his television. We were the only boys from Orangeburg at the time, two among a group of people labeled "country."

.   .

Morehouse was unlike anything we had ever seen. From the moment we walked on campus in downtown Atlanta, we knew we were someplace special. Large statues of black men stood throughout the campus, and dorms were more than a hundred years old. The school was founded in 1867 to teach children of former slaves to read and has grown to be one of the most prestigious, private, all-male educational institutions in the nation.

Freshman orientation constantly emphasizes the "Morehouse mystique," the school's legacy, and the "Morehouse man"—men like Martin Luther King Jr., Samuel L. Jackson, Spike Lee, Herman Cain, and others; we learned we are mayors, scientists, actors, top government officials, writers, politicians, and activists.

The institution is very careful about revealing what exactly are the ingredients of the school's successful Morehouse mystique, but part of it is raising a young black man's consciousness, from the moment he walks on the campus, drilling it into his head that he is someplace special, that he is part of a society that holds him up, and that he must make sure his fellow brothers do the same. It is the experience of going through something very challenging and coming out of it stronger and with tight bonds between those who supported you or struggled alongside you on that journey.

I remember something Henry Goodgame, an administrator at Morehouse, told us: "Regardless of whatever they said you can never do, you'll never be, you are coming to a place where we all know that you can succeed; if you give us an opportunity to use what we know, we will help you get it. If you want to be like a man on the street, you want to be dealing with drugs, then stay in the street, because there is a whole industry for that—go back out there; but if you want to be here and you want to be a leader for your race, a leader for a global society, then you've got to work with the formula that we have, that we know works."

The orientation ceremony is designed to be a sacred moment for the freshman. It's a rite of passage, and far more than dropping a kid off at college and helping him get his room straight. We all gather with our parents in the Martin Luther King Jr. International Chapel. It's a sight to see: about seven hundred young black men, all dressed alike in the school's colors, same black tie, same white button-down shirt, same pants, and same maroon blazer.

Dressing in uniform is not only ceremonial, but it's a key piece of the mystique. The idea is that you lose your individuality, developed in so many different hometowns, and become a class of men who are destined to lead. We dress like one unit, which says: it matters to me, your brother, that you are successful because you represent me, and I represent you.

During the ceremony, the administrators and students give powerful speeches, telling us to look to our right and left because we are in a room of greatness. This is a school, they say, where giants were groomed. As we look around, we see poor kids, rich kids, country boys, urbanites, former thugs, science nerds; there are international students, children of celebrities and kids of diplomats; there are people raised by struggling parents and everything in between. But we all have two things in common: we are black men, and we are all at the top of our classes. Exceptions to stereotype, we are all young black men who want to be serious students.

Of about four hundred kids at Orangeburg-Wilkinson High School, only about five boys, including me and Jarrod, were part of the top 25 percent of our class—the rest were girls. At Morehouse, hundreds of black boys graduated at the top of their classes.

During a parting ceremony, parents are told they have done the right thing. They are asked: "If you can't leave your son at Morehouse, where can you leave him? The streets are not safe; the world is not safe; but here, your son will build a network that will be to his advantage in the long term." We all leave the chapel, walking arm-in-arm with our parents toward the school's large gate. Once we get there, we are told to stop, and our parents are told to keep walking through the gate. While their backs are turned to us, the gate is closed and we head back to the chapel. By the time our parents turn around, we're walking away, leaving them as boys forever.

My mother says it hits parents right then and there that

their little boys are on their way to becoming men. "I cried as hard with Bakari as I did with Lumumba," she says.

• •

Once we shed the regalia, we could see how different we all were. There were the Houston boys, who wore only Polo boots. The DC guys wore only two to three colors—black, red, and blue—and they loved futuristic sneakers, like the Nike Air Foamposite, and hoodies. The Atlanta guys had their own dialect. And since they were on their own turf, they were comfortable wearing flip flops and socks. The New Yorkers wore massive white T-shirts and hats that were intentionally too big. They could be obnoxious because everything that came out of their mouths was "New York City." The Detroit guys, in their Coogi and Fat Albert sweaters, were the sharpest dressers of all. They tended to be suburban black kids with corporate executive parents who desperately wanted their sons to experience what it felt like to be around other African Americans.

Jarrod and I were "country." Our attire was a combination of ill-fitting clothes we once thought were cool—anything from Belk department store. We wore Nautica, Polo, and Tommy Hilfiger T-shirts and added a pair of khakis if we were trying to dress up.

Despite our outward differences, we all noticed that something was actually happening; the speeches and the way the administrators and older students carried themselves was quickly rubbing off on us. We were constantly told that we were part of a brotherhood built on helping each other achieve. We started to believe we were part of an environment where you stay woke, and it was our responsibility to keep our fellow brother awake so he didn't miss what's offered.

Something in the air encouraged mutual respect, but we were still very young with a lot to learn. On that orientation day, Jarrod and I met someone who'd be an important part of my Morehouse life from the first day to the last. The same way Jarrod started on me the day we met in high school, I started on Brandon Childs. He was from outside of Atlanta, not country but not city either.

Whereas people assume I'm a basketball player because of my height, there was nothing about Brandon that screamed baller. He was only six-foot-one, he wore glasses, and he was quiet. "He was a kind of lanky, kind of goofy kid, who liked to dance, and he wasn't boisterous," Jarrod recalls. So when Brandon told us he had a basketball scholarship at Morehouse, which was very rare, I started trash talking: "If somebody looking like you got a basketball scholarship, I know I can get one."

My trash talking never stopped until I saw Brandon on the court, dunking on people, shooting threes. He was a brilliant slasher, and he played defense. Morehouse didn't have a good deal of basketball success, but during the four years we were there, Brandon turned the team around. He was that good.

Brandon became a great friend, but Jarrod never let me live down my early comments to Brandon: "Of all the people Bakari chose to talk trash about, and literally on the first day of

Morehouse, is the guy who ends up becoming one of the stars in all the history of Morehouse basketball."

What made this especially funny to Jarrod is that there's an ongoing joke among my friends that I'm not as good of a basketball player as I think, despite my love for the game. Morehouse was a Division 2 team, and so there's a limited window for guys who want to try out for basketball. Jarrod never let me live down the fact that I didn't make the "walk on." "What's so funny is Bakari talks like he's really good, but he's not," Jarrod says. "I've been watching him play basketball for years. He's never been good. In his mind, he knows basketball, so in his mind he's good."

After I didn't make the walk on, Jarrod proceeded to report the fact to friends back home. He called Gavin Jackson, a high school classmate from Orangeburg. "You won't believe this," Jarrod said.

"What?" Gavin said.

"Man, that boy Sellers is trying to walk on to the basketball team."

Gavin was like, "Who's team? Spelman's?" (Spelman is Morehouse's adjacent women's college.)

Despite our mutual jabs, Jarrod's been someone I can always depend on, the truest example of brotherhood. He ended up running my successful political races in college as well as my run for a seat in South Carolina's House of Representatives. Still, it's humbling to have grown up in Denmark and to have a friend like Jarrod, who will always keep you in your place. It's probably the reason I'm not afraid to show my flaws to the world, and I'm sure Jarrod could say the same thing.

During those early days after freshman orientation, Jarrod and I found it easy to make friends. Jiving carried on into college, and our mastery of it made us stand out. In fact, many of the brothers at Morehouse were taken aback by our superior skills in the art of verbal warfare, especially when they tried to snap back. They soon learned we were slightly better. Often, another student would get exasperated and say, "Ah, y'all so country," and we'd own it, because we knew being called country at Morehouse was said out of brotherly love.

· ·

During our second month at Morehouse, two planes crashed into the Twin Towers in New York City on September 11, 2001. We woke up late that day, and Jarrod turned on his television to see the Twin Towers burning. We initially thought it was a terrible accident, but then we started hearing about terrorists. Of course, the only terrorists these two country boys had ever heard of were members of the Ku Klux Klan.

That day classes were canceled, and a few students had to leave campus and head home to the Northeast to be with their families. For some of us, it felt like the science fiction movie *Independence Day*, where aliens attack Earth. Still, many others felt safe in Atlanta, reasoning that no one would attack a majority *black* city—what would be the point of *that*? Somehow, things went on as usual.

Jarrod was as studious as ever, but I wasn't the best student, maybe because I was only sixteen, free of my parent's rule, and could get into any club I wanted to in Atlanta with a fake ID. My weekend started on Thursday and ended on Sunday night. And I was having the time of my life—until everything went sideways.

During my first semester, I was summoned to see the dean, who told me I was being placed on academic probation. Several months later, I lost my academic scholarship. I was also arrested on the campus of our sister school Spelman. I was sitting in Spelman's student center with a Spelman girl, and we were having so much fun that we forgot to keep an eye on the time. I looked up at the clock at around 10:30 p.m., past curfew, and then saw campus police officers rolling on me heavy, four cops deep. They escorted me off campus, and I was cited for trespassing and actions unbecoming of a Morehouse man.

There was more change to come. I started out as a pre-med student; my sister was a doctor, so I just figured I was going to be a doctor too. But that clearly wasn't a good fit. Because I had skipped grades when I was younger, math never clicked for me, and I didn't have any idea that so much math would be involved in my attempt to be a physician.

I eventually had a moment of introspection when I realized that I needed to find a major that would accept all of my credits because I wasn't going to be able to afford to stay for an extra year of school if I failed my first year. So I changed my major to African-American studies. Luckily, all my pre-med credits were accepted. My short adventure with the medical world had ended.

My brother Lumumba wonders whether it was a good idea

for my parents to skip both me and my older sister, who also went to college at age sixteen. He says that Nosizwe and I could be awkward children because we were always younger than all of our peers.

When I was younger, my sister and I had hilarious arguments about who was the smartest. Lumumba says, "They got the brains, but I got common sense." It's often said in our family that Nosizwe and I are different kinds of learners. She's a quick learner but had to study. Bakari, they say, could listen and comprehend what he heard.

Lumumba was a little different; he was always that person who thought things out. The summer before he was to attend Morehouse, he looked for work that would make him the most money for school but also provide him with enough physical activity to keep his body in shape for college football. The construction firm he chose coincidentally was the company my parents would hire to build our new home, a large brick ranch house on three to four acres of land. So when my brother returned home from school for Thanksgiving, he was able to live in a home he had built with his own hands, which he called one of the most spiritual moments of his life. He learned what it felt like to help make a brick-and-mortar reality out of something dreamed up on paper. The year before, he had decided he should work under a chef because he loved to cook. And he did just that. Now he's a minister and a sought-after tech executive. Whereas my sister and I pursued jobs that provided a service rather than the highest salaries, Lumumba did both.

· ·

Although my mother, especially, wasn't happy with what she was hearing about me in Atlanta—the girls, the partying, the fake IDs, and losing my scholarship—there was little my parents could do. They knew I wasn't going to fail in school because they had raised me early on to do the right thing, but still my mother was worried because, as she put it, I was "young and country."

Actually, I was dead set on building relationships and creating moments. This is what my parents always taught me, and this intentional parenting I received early on in life helped me to rebound from my mistakes.

My goal at Morehouse was to experience being a student, to find my passion—and I did. The job of a professor is to make students' brains sweat, to keep students on their toes with the best of research. My grades never got much better, hovering a bit under or exactly at a 3.0, but they never got worse either. I never skipped class, always did my work, and continued to learn, but my focus was no longer on making perfect grades. Rather, I was discovering new ideas, finding and experiencing my interests.

The summer following my freshman year, I was seventeen and wondering what to do. Jarrod had his summer already laid out. He was going to Washington, DC, to be an intern with the Congressional Black Caucus foundation at Congressman Jim Clyburn's office. I wanted that too, but when I tried to apply, I was told Clyburn's office was not going to sign another intern. So I called my mother. She's always relentless when she wants something or when she believes we need something. This is the woman who talked her way into a prison so my father could meet his baby daughter. When I told her my dilemma, she picked up the phone and called Jim Clyburn himself. (Congressman Clyburn was from Sumter, South Carolina, and he and my dad had been extremely close during the 1960s.)

"I want my son to be an intern," she said.

And they hired me.

I was paid $998 that summer. I stayed in Washington with my Aunt Florence (country folk pronounce "aunt" as "ain't" or "aintie"), my grandmother's sister. She lived in a beautiful brownstone near 14th and Kenyon Street NW, right across from an elementary school and a McDonalds.

I survived on the food provided at legislative receptions and whatever frozen scraps my great aunt had in the freezer. One of the special things she taught me, even at her age, was how to shave. I needed to learn to shave because I could afford to get a haircut only every other week and was beginning to have facial hair, which meant I didn't have that clean-cut look that was so common on Capitol Hill.

My dad was going to talk me through the process over the phone, but Dad used Magic Shave, which I didn't like. Number one, it stank and burned, and number two, the first time I tried to use it, I couldn't get all the gook off my face. Also, for some reason, my dad would shave his face with a butter knife—not an attribute I wanted to pick up from him. Luckily, Aunt Florence came through.

We walked to the bathroom where she showed me how to use warm water to wash my face, how to lather up, and how to put the shaving cream on my face. Then she got close to me and told me to pull my skin a little bit apart so I could have a regular surface and which direction to shave in. Every time I think about my first shave, I see my elderly aunt hovering over me.

· ·

Our family had a great deal of respect for Congressman Clyburn and his wife, whom we called Mrs. Emily. The two of them met in jail during the civil rights movement. She offered him some of her sandwich, and they have never been separated since.

The congressman had a friendly office with people who inspired me to eventually become a lawyer. One of the young men I met and worked with there was Jamie Harrison, who was a celebrity at Orangeburg-Wilkinson High School because he made it out of Orangeburg and went on to study at Yale. He worked for Congressman Clyburn during the day and attended Georgetown law school at night. There was Barvetta Singletary, who knew everything about health-care policy. All of us, including Jarrod, reported to Yelberton Watkins, the chief of staff, whom we affectionately called Yebbie. He was from Columbia, my state's capital.

Sometimes I would run errands for Yebbie, which included picking up his nieces from summer camp near Georgetown. He'd give me a little money, and I'd buy them ice cream before taking them back to the Capitol. I also responded to letters from constituents. Every now and then I'd get an opportunity to lead a tour at the Capitol and ride the underground shuttle, an old, electrical subway system linking the Capitol to the Senate and House buildings.

The most important thing I did was watch and learn from Congressman Clyburn himself. This was long before his successful bid for House Majority Whip in 2019. Back then, Clyburn had been in Congress for ten years. He was on the Appropriations Committee and had accumulated the respect and admiration of his colleagues.

When you walked into his office, you'd see all of these pictures on the wall of the Briggs family and their fight for educational justice. Harry and Eliza Briggs were plaintiffs in the 1952 *Briggs v. Elliott* case, which challenged desegregation in Summerton, South Carolina, and became the first of five cases that were combined in the famous *Brown v. Board of Education* effort decided by the US Supreme Court two years later.

There were two things you couldn't dismiss about Jim Clyburn: First, he was unapologetically black. He cared about issues that directly affected black folk. And second, he was a South Carolinian through and through. Contrary to popular belief, South Carolina produces more peaches than Georgia, and every year the South Carolina delegation distributes peaches to everyone in Congress. That summer, it was my and Jarrod's job to go around and deliver the peaches. We decided to give all the bruised peaches to Katherine Harris, the former Florida Secretary of State, who became infamous during the 2000 election debacle for certifying and awarding George Bush all of Florida's electors, giving him the presidency over Al Gore. She later became a Republican member of Congress. After getting our peaches, I bet Harris now knows South Carolina produces the most peaches, surely more than her state of Florida, but I'm pretty sure she doesn't like them!

Admittedly, Jarrod and I got caught up in the glitzy games of being congressional interns, but more importantly, we began believing that what we dreamed could come true. And whether it was the influence of Morehouse or the environment on Capitol Hill (it was probably both), we dreamed a lot that summer. It was easy to imagine we'd be successful, because we were seeing in DC leaders who looked like us and were doing what we wanted to do.

People often ask me what they can do to help a young person be a leader or to go out into the world to create change. And I say, when you're black, the number one thing you can do is to be an example. You can't tell a black kid to be a doctor if he's never seen a black doctor. You can't tell a black kid she can be a lawyer if she's never met a black lawyer. Jarrod and I were able to see what it was like to be a lobbyist, which is what he became, and a lawyer, which is what I am today. Through examples, we were able to imagine our future selves, and then we believed we could achieve those goals, even though we came from the isolated dirt roads of South Carolina.

IV

The Making of a Politician, Part 1

Parents often approach me and ask, "How were you able to do things at such a young age?" Or they try to compare their own sons to me. I tell them that we always find our niches, but at different times. I didn't really find my mission, so to speak, until that first summer after my troubled freshman year of college. I was seventeen years old when I started thinking about running for political office. Actually, it was during that summer in Congressman Clyburn's office on Capitol Hill that Jarrod and I formally plotted my run for South Carolina's House of Representatives. We had learned that running for office was a science, and we were thrilled that we could understand that science. We pulled data, spent hours and days searching voter registration websites, and investigated everything we knew could help us win in a few years.

We started examining my future opponent's record. Thomas Rhoad Jr. was, at the time, an eighty-year-old white man, a former farmer and milkman who had held the seat for more than twenty years. We studied the district lines he governed and who his constituents were, and we realized he was representing a district that was mostly black, including my hometown. We pored over his voting records, attempting to see what he'd done to help improve the area. What we found was what I already knew. The district was socially, economically, and educationally emblematic of a larger problem in South Carolina. We weren't growing, even slowly—we were declining.

Jarrod and I spent more time than one could ever imagine studying who voted for Rhoad and where they lived. We also dissected district lines over a twenty-year period. It would all pay off, but that year there was still much more to do.

When I returned to Morehouse as a sophomore, I was doing what I needed to do to get by, but I had been bit by the political bug. I wanted to build leadership experience, and so I ran for and won my first student government campaign that year. It was a basic college campaign—knocking on doors, putting up fliers.

But I made it a priority and purpose to cultivate relationships. In other words, I made sure that every single day, *I saw people*. I mean that in the truest sense of the word: whether it was the janitor, the cafeteria workers, or the president of the college, I always made sure that people knew that I *saw* them. I did the same with all my classmates, all my friends—all the people I came in contact with every day. It's a people skill my father and mother instilled in me, and it has real currency in politics.

I attempted to be affable, and my classmates awarded me by electing me junior class president. My second campaign, however, wasn't so easy. In fact, it was hell.

• •

That summer coming up to my junior year, in 2003, when I was eighteen, I lived in an apartment complex called the Villages of East Lake with five best friends: Anthony Locke, Rob Hewitt, Jason Mercer, Brian Fitch, and Brandon Childs. The housing in the area was predominately black and inhabited mostly by students. We had two three-bedroom condos that were side by side. That summer, I worked as an intern for the mayor's office in Atlanta, riding the MARTA, Atlanta's subway system, every day to work.

I can't recall whether I got paid for the internship, but I was scraping by financially. Since I no longer had a college scholarship, I was living off my refund checks, meaning I lived off whatever was left from my school loans. I'd write a bunch of cashier's checks for six months to cover rent, food, and other essentials. Everything left over had to be rationed, and I'd make it last.

The only food we had at the house were potatoes. I would enter the shared kitchen space at the mayor's office with my two potatoes, microwave them, grab a plastic fork, and then go hide in an office so no one could see me every day eating baked potatoes drizzled with ranch dressing.

Despite my lack of funds that summer, what I learned back then was priceless. In fact, both Jim Clyburn and Shirley Franklin, then the mayor of Atlanta, inspired my first political slogan: "It's not about politics but about public service."

The mayor had attended Howard University with my dad. He always called her by her maiden name, Shirley Clark, so I never knew who he was talking about. Though she couldn't be more than five feet tall, Mayor Franklin was a giant. She demanded and commanded respect, but she would always give it back, too. Strangers would stop her on the sidewalks in Atlanta, bending down to give her a big hug. Shirley Franklin dressed to the nines every day, and like the black women of a generation before her, she always wore a fresh flower instead of a brooch.

Atlanta is a city that's run by nothing but black folk, and sometimes we allow our petty differences to get in the way of governance. But from my point of view, the mayor was not that way. Instead, Mayor Franklin focused on what was important to the citizens of Atlanta. She never chose sexy issues. For instance, she passionately worked on repairing the water system in the city, which might not be sexy, but it directly affected everyone.

One thing I learned from working on Capitol Hill with Jim Clyburn, and in the mayor's office with Shirley Franklin, is that the lifeblood of politics is very simple: relationships.

Me and my boys had already built a huge alliance, and our notoriety derived from the fact that we were all part of different groups; we built a consensus of very popular and influential people on campus. Brandon Childs was a basketball player. Jarrod, though not living with us that summer, was a rising leader among the Alpha Phi Alpha fraternity, one of the traditional and historically black fraternities on campus.

I wasn't part of any group but was friendly with everyone. The editor-in-chief of the college newspaper was one of my good friends, and the basketball captain was one of my boys. Like any other school, Morehouse had different crowds—the business guys, the athletes, the fraternity guys, the nerds, the international students, and the gay students. I was friends with all of them.

That summer me and my boys were also known for our epic parties. Atlanta has always drawn black students from all over the country. In the late 1980s and 1990s, caravans of college students traveled to Atlanta for "Freaknik," a massive block party of up to two hundred thousand students who would spend $20 million in the city. The young people obviously felt comfortable coming to a city where the people in power looked like them. Another draw was that Atlanta boasted four historically black colleges: Morehouse, Spelman, Morris Brown, and Clark Atlanta University.

And all their students seemed to show up at our parties that summer of 2003. We didn't have a lot of money to buy alcohol, so we had to make our drinks stretch. We'd cook up a concoction of Hi-C, fruit cocktail, and 190-proof Everclear, which we marinated overnight in a cooler. We laid plastic on the floor, and I used my Nissan Sentra, which my sister had bought me for my birthday, to break the wood barrier at our apartment complex's entrance gate. With no barrier, a dozen cars could flow in at once.

By the end of the evening, about one hundred students had come through. Strangely enough, in those years, neighbors rarely called the police on us.

. .

Politics at Morehouse was serious. Brothers were giving speeches, going over campaign plans; dudes were creating real strategy—I loved everything about it. So in my junior year, and with all the confidence in the world, I threw my hat in the ring for Student Government Association (SGA) president. That decision to run for the top political position on campus made no sense to some people, especially the "SGA guys."

Remember, this is a college bred on leadership. It started with Benjamin E. Mays, the late educator, an intellectual, and the longtime president of Morehouse. Son of former slaves, Mays and his extraordinary story influenced some of the greatest civil rights leaders of our time, including Julian Bond, Andrew Young, and especially Martin Luther King Jr., who was only fifteen years old when he arrived at Morehouse. His father and grandfather had also attended the school.

Dr. King said of his life on campus: "My days in college were very exciting ones. There was a free atmosphere at Morehouse, and it was there I had my first frank discussion on race. The professors were not caught in the clutches of state funds and could teach what they wanted with academic freedom. They encouraged us in a positive quest for a solution to racial ills. I realized that nobody there was afraid. Important people came to discuss the race problem rationally with us."

At the time, Dr. King determined to be a lawyer, rather than a minister, revolting "against the emotionalism of much Negro religion. The shouting and stamping. I didn't understand it, and it embarrassed me." He questioned whether religion could be intellectually respectable as well as emotionally satisfying. But two people at Morehouse inspired him to give ministry a chance. He wrote that Dr. Mays and Dr. George Kelsey, a professor of philosophy and religion, "made me stop and think. Both were ministers, both deeply religious, and yet both were learned men, aware of all the trends of modern thinking. I could see in their lives the ideal of what I wanted a minister to be."

At Morehouse, I too attempted to lay the groundwork for my future as a leader. "Leadership" is an interesting term, because there is no clear definition, but people always define a leader as someone who has followers or someone dripping with charisma. I disagree with that wholeheartedly. For me, a good leader is someone who begets other leaders. It doesn't make sense if I have followers who are not leaders themselves. However, if I'm doing my job correctly, then other leaders will be with me, will listen to me, and then will go out and lead others. That's what I learned from Morehouse.

Martin Luther King Jr. entered the ministry his senior year at Morehouse. My "uncle" Julian Bond, who was a living legend himself during most of my lifetime, also attended Morehouse and remembered King and Mays when he was a student.

He described Mays as the quintessential Morehouse man: "He held up a standard of what a Morehouse man should be, and we wanted so badly to come up to that standard."

A wordsmith and brilliant orator who spoke at chapel every Tuesday, Mays was King's intellectual father and model. He would also, sadly, come to eulogize King on campus. Uncle Julian often recalled being one of eight students who took the only class King ever taught at Morehouse. He loved to say, "I am one of the eight people in the universe who can truly say 'I was a student of Martin Luther King.'" He often recalled seeing King in grocery stores and banks in Atlanta, and then of course later in Selma and the March on Washington.

Few people know that the actor Samuel L. Jackson, a sophomore at Morehouse in 1968, was an usher at King's funeral. King's death shook him and led him to activism. Jackson was expelled from Morehouse a year later after he and other student activists locked up the school's trustees in a building for two days. One of the board members was King's own father.

For a young black man eager to be a future leader, being at Morehouse was equivalent to being a young politician living in Boston or Philadelphia shortly after the Declaration of Independence was signed. There were men who came to Morehouse because they wanted to follow in the paths of these great black leaders. Others arrived at the school with the intention of becoming SGA president. That is how prestigious the position was in a school known to have bred some of the greatest trailblazers in US history. But that wasn't my interest. I just thought Morehouse could do some cool things for a larger population on and off campus.

Jarrod always said people underestimated my chances of winning the SGA presidency. "There were a lot of Morehouse guys who felt like they were entitled to be SGA president because they had been student trustees," he says. "Or they had been correspondent secretary in the previous administration, but this guy, Bakari, clearly didn't give a damn about any of that. It was clear to students that his world wasn't confined to the SGA world. Instead, he always had a broad-base reach at Morehouse."

The SGA election was packed with talented classmates, such as Lee Merritt, now a preeminent civil rights attorney who has represented women who have accused R. Kelly of sexual abuse and fought against police misconduct and white supremacy. I also ran against Clark Jones, a well-known comedian. But despite all my talented opponents, I still thought I could win. Through winning junior class president, I knew that knocking on every door and building a huge network of support was a winning formula.

I did win the SGA race, but that was just the first round of a long and hellish election. We had to move my first win to a runoff, because I didn't get 50 percent of the vote. Then I won the runoff too—which is when I was summoned to the dean's office. The mother of one of my opponents, who I will not name, called the then–vice president of Student Services Dean Bryce and told him the polls had opened up thirty minutes late. The woman claimed that was an "equal disadvantage," which I had never heard of in my life. Dean Bryce said the school was taking away my election victory; the entire election had to be done over again.

I stormed out of his office and called my dad. He knew how hard I had been working on that race. We had knocked on dormitory doors. We had gotten the support of every basketball player we could muster and all the fraternity friends I had. My friends Jarrod, Brian, Jason, Rob, Brandon, and Anthony helped me to galvanize the entire student body.

I remember about twenty of us marching into a meeting in the freshman dorm called the Living Learning Center. "We're all supporting Bakari Sellers. We need you to vote for him tomorrow!" We were like a mob, lobbying from one building to another, rolling deep and trying to connect with everyone we knew. We wanted to inspire people with our enthusiasm and energy, but also let them know, This is where you want to be, and these are the people you need to roll with.

We had ignited that kind of energy, but when Dean Bryce took that election from me, I was just sad. My dad suggested I call Julian Bond, who was then chair of the board at Morehouse. I believed we had a few things in common. Julian's father was a widely respected educator and college president. We both grew up around legends. There are childhood photos of me in the arms of well-known American groundbreakers, and there are extraordinary pictures of Julian Bond in the arms of the great Paul Robeson and W. E. B. Du Bois. And if anyone knew about early political setbacks, it was Uncle Julian.

So I called Julian Bond, pacing back and forth and crying, telling him what had happened. In a soothing voice, he comforted me, saying, "It's all going to work." When he was elected to the Georgia House of Representatives in 1965 at the age of twenty-six, his colleagues refused to seat him because he wouldn't apologize for anti-Vietnam sentiments that fellow SNCC members had recently made. In response, Martin Luther King Jr. openly criticized the House members and led a protest to the statehouse.

The US Supreme Court sided with Uncle Julian, who'd eventually serve four terms in the Georgia House and ten more years in the Senate. He also became chairman of the NAACP and founder of the Southern Poverty Law Center. But in 1985, he lost a race for Atlanta's Fifth District congressional seat, a seat he helped to create. Worst of all, he lost it to friend and civil rights comrade John Lewis, who was a city councilman at the time. The contest turned them into foes, with Lewis demanding that Uncle Julian take a drug test, which he refused because he said it was an invasion of privacy. If Lewis had run a more straightforward campaign, I believe, the US congressman from that district probably would have been Julian Bond rather than John Lewis.

Back in my apartment, a friend of mine named Lodriguez Murray, who now works for the United Negro College Fund, watched me pacing back and forth. After I hung up with Uncle Julian, Lodriguez pulled me aside and said, "You're just going to have to beat them all again."

The election was set for a week later, and I won the general election once again, which went into another runoff, which

I also won, though I had to persuade everybody who voted for me to vote for me for a fourth time! This struggle taught me many lessons and prepared me for the future. I learned at an early age that there are no permanent friends, no permanent enemies, just permanent interests. I also learned to keep grinding. My parents taught me that you have to run faster, jump higher, and work harder—and so I did.

Years later, Jarrod reflected on why I continued to win the SGA spot despite all the setbacks. "Your campaign team was your homeboys—it was us," he said. "And just by the virtue of your personality, you knew guys from every walk of life, and I think ultimately that's why people were drawn to you. I think that was your first real foray into electoral politics."

That summer after the SGA win, we accomplished some important things both on and off campus. Off campus, we conducted HIV and AIDS testing in Atlanta, where instances of HIV are extremely high. On campus, I turned my attention to the women who worked in the cafeteria. During my junior and senior years, I was not on a meal plan because I couldn't afford one. The only reason I ate at all was because the cafeteria ladies gave me free food. When we discovered that these women were making minimum wage, we fought diligently and successfully with the administration to get them higher wages. I owed them that much. We also promoted a homecoming concert featuring the rapper Lil Wayne.

During my senior year, I roomed again with Jarrod, who was now the president of the Alpha Phi Alpha fraternity, which placed him on the top of the social ladder at school. And of course I was the SGA president. These were two of the highest profile roles on campus, and they were being held by two Low Country boys. Jarrod was headed to graduate school at New York University, and then the Kennedy School at Harvard University, and I decided to go to law school. I knew that to get into law school I had to have at least three of four things: (1) a very high grade point average, which I didn't have; (2) a great résumé; (3) a great story (personal statement); and (4) excellent references. I applied to the law school at the University of South Carolina and was accepted, but I also had another goal I needed to tend to.

• •

After I graduated from Morehouse College in May 2005, when I was twenty, I went back home to live with my parents for the summer and to prepare for law school, which would start that August. But of course I had this master plan in my head, one that I had started drawing up that summer in Congressman Clyburn's office with Jarrod. So in June 2005, I made the decision to run in the next Democratic Party primary against Thomas Rhoad for South Carolina's House of Representatives, and it was time to tell my parents about my plans. I sauntered down the steps, very confident in what I was about to say.

In our kitchen, we have a cook island to the right and a wet bar to the left. I stood between the wet bar and the island. My mom, on one of her rare cooking days, was fixing spaghetti, and my dad was going through the newspapers. Being a millennial, I couldn't then, and can't now, understand for the life of me why older people read the newspaper at the end of the day. In any event, I needed to get his attention.

"Mom, Dad, I'm going to run for the South Carolina House against Thomas Rhoad," I said.

My mother turned to me without hesitation and said, "I will vote for you."

My dad, with somewhat of a snicker, put the paper down and said, "I will think about it."

V

The Making of a Politician, Part 2

In 2005 Thomas Rhoad was an eighty-two-year-old Democratic Party stalwart who had served in the statehouse for twenty-four years—longer than I'd been alive. Born in Bamberg County in 1923, he was a World War II veteran, a farmer, had served on the county council, and had been a mail deliverer. There wasn't anyone that he didn't know.

However, some things made me think Rhoad was politically vulnerable. For instance, he was an older white man in a district that was majority African American. A lot of people were waiting on Rhoad to retire—a waiting game that reminded me of how so many people sat on the sidelines waiting too long for the long-serving US senator from South Carolina Strom Thurmond to retire.

My family had been in the community for seventy-five years,

but something bigger than that cemented the idea that I must run. South Carolina's "Corridor of Shame," a region around I-95 where schools are not only poorly performing, but dilapidated, impoverished, and falling apart, runs right through the district. I thought of my friend Pop, and all the people I played ball with and grew up with and broke into the gym with in Denmark who were still there doing a lot of the same things— not because they didn't want to do anything different but because there was no opportunity for them to do anything else. I figured that I had an incredible chance to create prospects.

The first thing I did was buy a marble composition notebook at CVS and write down the names of people I needed to meet. One of the first people I set out to connect with was former South Carolina governor Dick Riley. After securing a meeting and entering his law office, I saw he didn't have anything on his desk, which made me wonder how much law he was practicing. Riley, a native of Greenville, which was part of the Upstate, or Upcountry as it's sometimes called, was a legend in South Carolina. President Bill Clinton had tried to appoint him to the Supreme Court in 1993, but Riley refused, and the seat went to Ruth Bader Ginsburg. But later that year, the governor did become Clinton's secretary of education.

I had known Riley since I was a child. In fact, most of the people I first went to see I knew through my father and from attending all those Orangeburg Massacre events when I was a little boy. I'd ring them up and say, "Hey, this is Little Cleve," or "This is Little CL."

Riley was on the phone when I walked in, so I sat down

and waited. Soon enough, I noticed he was talking to Marian Wright Edelman, the famous children's rights activist. "Marian, I'll call you back," he told her. "I have Bakari Sellers in here to chat with me for a little while."

When he hung up the phone, I asked, "Was that *the* Marian Wright Edelman?"

"Yeah, that's who that was," he said. It was a surreal moment for me.

What I love about Dick Riley is that he believes in the new generation. He loved my father and saw me as a younger version of him. Riley set a clear goal for me: "Make your dad and the state proud," he said. His advice was simple and reassuring, so simple I could breathe and run with it.

My mother also used her connections to arrange for me to meet with a large advertising firm in Columbia called Chernoff Newman. I sat down with Rick Silver, one of the firm's partners, who talked to me about marketing and my political platform. I told him I wanted to run on taking down the Confederate flag. He didn't push back on that idea, but he pointed out other things that I could run on as well. For instance, South Carolina still had extremely concerning issues, such as poverty and health care, that were directly affecting everyone. From those meetings I developed a campaign platform that emphasized quality education for your kids along with first-class health care for your grandparents—no matter if you were black or white.

As I scratched names off in my marble notebook, I knew I had a strict timeline to follow. I wasn't going to publicly announce my candidacy until September 18, 2005, because that was the day I turned twenty-one, and I couldn't be on the ballot until I was legally considered an adult.

I also learned that not everyone was going to believe in my dream. For example, one of the first people I met before announcing was Darrell Jackson—a great family friend, a megachurch pastor, and a South Carolina politician. My father helped Darrell get his start, hiring him to assist Jesse Jackson during Jesse's presidential runs in 1984 and 1988, but Darrell broke my heart. I thought that he would be outwardly effusive and supportive; I thought he would endorse me. I think my family did too, but instead, when I told him of my plan to run against Rhoad, he cautioned me not to do that. "You should run for school board or something," he told me. "Get your name out there first."

In my young mind at the time, I believed Darrell was throwing cold water on my dreams. Was that devastating or disrespectful? Not at all. I think that his advice was probably sound under most circumstances. But I didn't believe my first race to the statehouse, the race that would make history, was "most circumstances."

Now I would say that most of us millennials get a perverse sense of affirmation when we prove people wrong. So although I was disappointed in the conversation with Darrell simply because he didn't say what I wanted to hear, it motivated me. I wanted people to be supportive of my dream, but some of his comments made me realize that my youth was going to be an issue.

No disrespect to Senator Darrell Jackson, who to this day remains a friend and mentor, but I wasn't about to wait my turn. I think he probably realized later that it wasn't a typical conversation with a typical candidate, because I was Cleve Sellers' boy—that is, I was going to go out and be that radical change, regardless.

One of the coolest and more interesting preannouncement meetings I had was with State Senator John Matthews, who was not only a black Democrat in my district but also someone extremely supportive of my political opponent Rhoad. And it wasn't happenstance that Matthews picked Waffle House to talk politics.

In South Carolina, you go to the Waffle House to launch a political career or to grab a bite after you leave the strip club—and everything in between. Waffle Houses are more than a southern tradition; they're a southern staple. They're always open, they never let you down. My favorite meal is grilled pork chops with hash browns smothered with onions. In the South, Waffle House is also a reliable weather barometer. Hurricane warnings are nothing new in my home state, but if Waffle House closes its doors, you'd better evacuate!

Still, I admit I was hesitant about meeting Senator Matthews there, because you also smell like Waffle House when you leave.

I can't remember whether I ordered anything, but he had an egg sandwich on white bread with a cup of coffee. The conversation was quick. Matthews was always somebody I looked up to. I wanted him to know that I was running, although the purpose of that conversation was not necessarily to get him to support me. Instead, I was making sure I humbled myself enough to get him to stay out of the race, meaning that he would not come out and *outwardly support* my opponent.

"I have a great deal of respect for, and I know you have a great deal of respect for, Representative Rhoad," I told him. You always want to make sure to respect your opponent, because you're never sure in politics how much your opponent over twenty years had helped the person you're sitting across the table from. I asked Matthews for his guidance, which didn't necessarily require him to do much. Now I did want him to give me some words of wisdom, but even more importantly I wanted him to stay out of my race. So then I just said it: "Can you do me a favor and not get involved in this race? I know that you can't support me, but don't hurt me. If you can please do me a favor and stay out, I would greatly appreciate it."

Matthews sipped his coffee. Then he said, "Of course. I can do that."

As any shrewd politician would do, I'm sure Matthews probably told Rhoad he would support him and maybe even did some things for him. But he wasn't as harmful to me as he could have been if I hadn't had that Waffle House conversation.

• •

I started law school in August. Meanwhile, Jarrod was calling all our classmates from Morehouse and Spelman and raising money. They were sending me ten and twenty dollars at a time via online fundraising websites. The way to raise money in politics is far simpler than you could ever imagine. People always tell me, "But I don't know any special interest groups." Well, I didn't either. And if I did, they were supporting my opponent. I also heard a lot of, "None of my friends have money." Well, none of my friends had money either.

I began my campaign with the only money I could scrounge, which started with a one-thousand-dollar check from my mother. My campaign ran off that money for the first month. My mom and dad have handwritten address books they break out for graduations, deaths, and weddings. I started sending letters to people in their books, using my letterhead and stamps and envelopes I bought. I contacted every single person in my family and everyone on the list I made, maybe two hundred people, people who were invited to my graduation and otherwise. I simply wrote, "I am running for office and I need your help."

My parents raised me to understand the value of a dollar. For instance, I especially appreciated and placed a high value on, say, a twenty-five-dollar check from an older church lady. I knew her money had great value because once she wrote a check, which likely came from her retirement, she was invested in my winning. She'd call her friends and stand up in church and remind everyone to vote for me. That's how I raised money, from people who gave small amounts but were completely invested.

The primary election was scheduled for June 13, 2006, which meant we had nine months to run the race. I believed that gave us enough time to do everything we needed to do. Now, I always refer to campaigns as "we" and "us," even if it's just me knocking on a door. Whenever someone asks whether I'm considering running for something, I always say, "We are thinking about it." The reason is simply because campaigns are about more than just the one person running.

I called Thomas Rhoad before making my announcement. I felt like that was the appropriate thing to do, but he never called me back. In fact, I never spoke with him once throughout the campaign until two days after I won. During the entire race, I ran against an opponent who I would always treat with respect, but I don't know whether he respected me or not.

Anton Gunn, a young black man who also ran for office in 2006, was on my list of people to talk to and would later be important to President Obama's 2008 candidacy. Anton had lunch with me one day at Harpers, in Columbia. He is six-foot-five and about three hundred pounds, a former star offensive lineman for the University of South Carolina. My father, who was a professor there for nearly two decades, was Anton's adviser. Anton, soft-spoken and smart as a whip, destroys every stereotype one might have of an imposing athlete.

He, in turn, introduced me to Kendall Corley, a brilliant political consultant. I hired Kendall and probably paid him mere hundreds a month. He's a consultant extraordinaire now, but when I met him, Kendall didn't have any races under his belt. However, he could "cut maps." He was brilliant at it, like a mad scientist figuring out through data and studying maps where I should knock on doors.

Finally, on September 18, 2005, my twenty-first birthday, I held my niece in my arms outside the old train depot in Denmark and announced my candidacy. Only one reporter was there, along with family members and church folk who attended our family church, St. Philip's Episcopal. I don't know whether they thought I could win, but I knew they believed in me. From that day on, I started knocking on doors.

On Fridays, Saturdays, and Sundays, I'd knock on about four hundred doors, and every other day I'd knock on only one hundred. Most of the time, I was out there by myself, but sometimes volunteers joined me. Kendall made sure we hit the right areas.

I knew we were gaining traction when we had volunteers go back and knock on the same doors. One man who lived in Norway finally came to the door. "I'm going to vote for him," he said, "but if you knock on my door one more time, I'm a vote for the other person."

I'd often go door knocking after a law class. I'd grab a map, put on a pair of slacks and a campaign shirt, and walk and knock. It didn't matter to me if there was a Confederate flag in the yard; I was still knocking on that door. If a house had a pit bull in the front yard, I'd creep around to the back on tip toe and try to knock on the back door. I met mothers who gave me lemonade and cookies and introduced me to their daughters. And I met people who told me, "Go to hell, I'll never vote for a Democrat in my lifetime."

Banging on doors is tedious, but it's a necessary political exercise—one that new politicians often don't practice. Not doing it, though, is the quickest way to get beat. People think all you do is raise money and pay for TV ads, but where I'm from, door-to-door retail, old school Jimmy Carter politics is still important.

When you knock on a door, you feel a mini-rush. You never know what's on the other side, you never know how you're going to be received. All you have is a formulaic greeting and campaign literature that you make sure to leave behind. But you see and meet everyone in their natural element. When people come to the door, they can be shirtless, in boxers and church socks. Or they can be preparing for their next day or going to bed—the key is that you're meeting people where they are.

At the end of the day, I was always tired, because I walked miles. My black church shoes had holes so big I could stick two fingers through the soles and touch the ball of my foot.

Most people were cordial. Even staunch racists usually won't say to your face what they feel. I'd get calls at the house saying, "Tell that nigga to get out of the race," but no one said that to me personally. On Election Day, at the voting precinct in East Denmark, a man did try to intimidate voters. He got out of his truck with a shotgun but then got back in his truck. I wanted to win a race, so I couldn't let such things stop me.

I spent nine months knocking on doors and also visiting black churches—a different one each Sunday. My goal was to touch everybody three times: knock on their door, send them a piece of mail, and speak to them on their phone. Mailing and phoning cost money, but knocking just costs time. So that's what I did, all through the district, which included Bamberg County, Springfield, Norway, and the southern part of Orangeburg.

Then there was a real small part of Barnwell, which I don't think had ten black voters in that part of town. It was called Hilda. Someone said, "You have to go to Hilda, and you have to go to this country store, and then you have to go in and meet people and shake hands there." So my one campaign event in Hilda was to visit that store, shake hands, tell people I was running for office—and eat a thirty-five-cent mayonnaise sandwich offered to me by the kind storeowners. I have this real bad reaction to mayonnaise; it's not an allergy, but I hate it. I took one bite of that sandwich anyway and chased it down with some sweet tea: this is politics too.

A friend from Morehouse moved to Columbia and campaigned with me every single day. Although Jarrod was now in graduate school at NYU, he was all strategy, making sure we were doing the right things. Kendall navigated me to knock on all the right doors. But, of course, not everyone was helpful. Representative Gilda Cobb-Hunter was a great friend of Thomas Rhoad, and so she went out of her way to campaign for him in churches in my district. I had my Bakari Sellers sign in front of my house in my yard, but Rhoad's people placed his signs on each side of my signs—in my own yard! Cobb-Hunter wanted to cut my ass, but that's just politics. In fact, she's a wildly effective legislator, someone I later worked diligently to get in her good graces. In fact, I've patterned my own political career after hers.

I won only eight of thirty precincts in June 2006, but those districts were large and were many of the ones Jarrod and I had picked out when I was seventeen. As we estimated, those districts were enough to give me the edge I needed to win. At the age of twenty-one, I won my first election, and while still enrolled in law school (now age twenty-two), I took my seat as the youngest-ever member of South Carolina's House of Representatives. My mother held the Bible as I was sworn in.

I entered the statehouse complex every day knowing I was walking into one of the most beautiful capitol buildings in the nation. There are twenty-two monuments on the grounds of the statehouse in downtown Columbia. One honors Strom Thurmond, the late segregationist, who was both beloved and despised in my state. His monument was altered in 2004 to include the name of Essie Mae Washington-Williams, a retired African American teacher who was Thurmond's oldest daughter by an African American maid who worked for his family.

The grand entrance of the statehouse is lined by twenty-two giant columns, all carved from one piece of granite. Six bronze stars are attached on the outside walls, positioned to cover the holes made by General William T. Sherman and his Union troops, who blasted the statehouse with cannon fire in 1865, the year slavery was abolished.

A beautiful dome, covered with forty-four-thousand pounds of copper, sits atop the building. The Confederate flag flew above the dome since 1961 to mark the centennial anniversary of the start of the Civil War, and it also remained there as a snub to the civil rights movement. Lawmakers compromised in 2000, removing the flag from above the dome to a thirty-foot pole next to the Confederate monument in front of the statehouse.

In the back of my mind I always had thought that a deal to take the flag off the top of the dome and put it in the front of the statehouse was just not a good deal. I never thought the flag would come down, but I was resolved from the beginning that we would try our damnedest.

During my early months in office, I received a call from Anton Gunn, at that time the only member of Barack Obama's South Carolina election campaign. After coming up short in his own statehouse election, Anton did something that would help change the course of South Carolina's election history. He landed the job of running Obama's South Carolina campaign by sitting in the then-senator's DC office and persuading him of the unthinkable: he could help Obama win the South Carolina primary.

It would not be an easy task. Hillary and Bill Clinton had a lot of political cachet built among older black elected officials, going back to the 1990s. For example, Darrell Jackson had run Bill Clinton's presidential campaign in South Carolina more than twenty years earlier. But younger African Americans didn't have such ties to the Clintons; I surely didn't.

On the phone, Anton got right to the point: "We need you to endorse Barack Obama for president."

"Man, I don't know," I said. At the time, I had narrowed my choices down to Obama and North Carolina senator John Edwards but was leaning heavily toward Edwards. "Nobody's talking about poverty like Edwards, and he's from around here," I said. "He's handsome, and his campaign headquarters are going to be in the ninth ward," which was and still is the epitome of black New Orleans.

Edwards had a platform built around the haves and the have-nots. Unlike most people, who talked only about rural white America, Edwards talked also about the black poor in my community, like those folk who had to ride on a bus for hours each day to work menial jobs. I was impressed by him, though I also felt that something didn't quite feel right about him. But like everyone else, I was bamboozled and couldn't see through his veneer. (Edwards was indicted in 2011 for misusing campaign funds to cover up an extramarital affair.)

Something Anton said on that call, however, prevented me from making a bad decision: "You will never have to explain your endorsement of Barack Obama."

I still wasn't ready to endorse Obama, but that comment made me realize that my constituents could understand why someone like me, a black man and an elected official, would.

VI

Dreaming with My Eyes Open
Becoming a Leader

I was walking to my constitutional law class in April 2007 when I got a call from Barack Obama himself.

That morning, a private phone number showed up on my cell phone. I'm terrified of private numbers because it can be one of two people: somebody very important, or somebody working for a student loan company trying to get their money back. That day, it turned out to be the former. "Do you have a moment to speak to Senator Obama?," I was asked.

I was shocked, but maybe I shouldn't have been. "I do," I said.

Winning the seat that Thomas Rhoad had dominated for nearly a quarter of a century certainly made me a surprise and a political upset in my home state, but I was getting attention from people outside of Denmark and even beyond South Carolina. With the southern primaries for Democratic presidential elections looming, and my home state being the first of them, candidates in my party began courting me to endorse them. Hillary Clinton and Joe Biden had already called. All this was happening during my first year of law school at the University of South Carolina.

Still, I didn't make my decision to officially endorse Obama until he called me that morning as I was leaving my office in the statehouse. With my book bag in tow, I started on my usual two-block trek to class—which involved walking past the coffee shop on my right and Miyo's Asian cuisine on my left. Once a week I'd stop at Sandy's for a slaw-dog with chili. Then I'd head to class and return to the statehouse in the early afternoon.

That morning, Senator Obama asked me what was going on and what was I doing. I told him I was on my way to my constitutional law class. I'd like to think I'm wittier than that, but I had a brain freeze. My constitutional law professor was a great scholar, a fine Democrat, and a good liberal, but I remembered nothing she had taught me at that moment.

Senator Obama, a constitutional law expert, started peppering me with questions that I just didn't know the answers to. He wanted to know where we were in our studies and what cases we were looking at. Finally, he said, "Now is the time that I want you to endorse me for president of the United States."

"Senator," I said, "I will do so under two conditions: one, my mom gets an opportunity to volunteer for your campaign. And two, you visit my district."

"I have no problem with doing either of those," he said.

My mom was no longer working as a professor at South Carolina State, and I felt her volunteering would get her out of the house. Indeed, she became a steady volunteer for the Obama campaign, but the mystery for me was whether Obama would make good on his word about my other request. Would he really come to Bamberg County? I'd have to wait and see.

Meanwhile, I was becoming increasingly acclimated to my new legislative position. As I'd walk up the fifty-two steps of the statehouse during those early days and months, my twenty-two-year-old self often would be thinking and psyching myself up: *I'm about to shake some shit up at the capitol! This millennial is going to go in there and wobble the foundation of racism and bigotry and classism and inequality!*

In my heart, I was going to go in there and fix everything. That, of course, wasn't necessarily going to be the case. In fact, I soon realized that my job was actually the definition of insanity—it was where I went to work trying every single day to do just that, but nothing changed.

In a photograph taken of me on my first day of session, I'm looking up at the ceiling. The photograph made the *Los Angeles Times*, which wrote about my race making history. The moment that photograph was taken, I was thinking to myself, *I can't believe I'm here!* But by January, I was looking around at members of South Carolina's General Assembly and thinking, *I can't believe* you're *here.*

It was shocking to me that some of those people had been in office for years upon years, but they were not in the mode of service. Some were more concerned about daily receptions than they were about governing. And there were receptions every night, every breakfast, and every lunch. There was always lots of food and drink. The receptions allowed citizens from various groups (for example, insurance, the Farm Bureau, associations for the blind, or the PTA) to spend time in Columbia with their elected officials, and it allowed us to spend time with our constituents.

I felt I belonged in the House chambers. No matter how long my fellow members had been there, regardless of how old they were, I knew that we all represented the people. My constituents had sent me to the statehouse just like their constituents had sent them. Still, my being a young black Democrat in a deeply red state made it tough.

And yet, being in the General Assembly was nothing less than amazing. As I look back over my eight years as an elected official, I realize I was lucky to have served among so many superstars. Since I was in South Carolina, they were mostly Republican stars, but stars nonetheless, like Jeff Duncan, now a US congressman; and Nikki Haley, who'd become the governor of South Carolina and later US ambassador to the United Nations. I served with Tim Scott, one of the few black US senators, and Mick Mulvaney, later a congressman who also served in President Donald Trump's cabinet. Mick was in my freshman class of the newly elected state legislators.

Since I was so young, a lot of pressure was on me. I knew everything I said would be scrutinized; I knew everyone wondered, Who is this young man from Denmark? What's all the fuss about? What's he going to say? But as I had done my entire life, I made sure that I was more prepared than the next person. Every morning I scoured the news, from periodicals to blogs, just to make sure I understood every important ongoing issue. I tried to attend committee meetings and even sat in on committees I wasn't part of. These meetings helped me to measure the dynamics of the statehouse. I also wanted to be friends with people on both sides of the aisle so that I could become more effective in my very red state. I realized quickly that, alone, there are no superheroes. People have to learn basic math, which is to say, with 124 representatives, it was clear that my magic number was always 63 to pass a vote.

I was fascinated to come to understand how political deals are made. To be an effective legislator, you need to know that deals are never struck inside the chambers; they are never agreed to in committee meetings. The receptions aren't where the sausage is made either. Rather, we practically lived in Columbia's Sheraton and Hilton hotels, where we'd sit down at the bar in the lobbies to talk. Frankly, that's where everything got done—undercover, usually over a glass of vodka and soda, and where we were able to be human beings and not performance politicians.

I'm talking about groups of maybe twenty elected officials. There, we learned about each other's families, about spouses and kids. We laughed and joked and stayed up till 1 a.m. It didn't matter if you were black or white, Democrat or Republican. We came together to at least try to get a few things done, which was hard for someone like me—young, black, and Democrat.

Of course, I especially wanted to make sure I befriended the Black Caucus members. Some of them I knew growing up in the area and through my father, and others I got to know over time. I relied heavily on those veteran members of the caucus, and I ended up being somebody who challenged them as much as they challenged me to slow down and pay attention. It was a learning experience both ways. I think I added some value to their work by helping them understand the importance of social media and the relevance of the Black Lives Matter movement, but they definitely added a significant value to my eight years in office too. One Black Caucus member, Lonnie Hosey, was a mentor to me. A former Marine and Vietnam veteran, he had been wounded in action and earned a Purple Heart. You didn't want to make Lonnie angry, but he was somebody you'd want to be in a foxhole with.

Lonnie used to sit next to Seth Whipper, another Black Caucus member, whose mother had also served in the House. Both men unfortunately had lost their sons, and perhaps in some way I filled a void for them. When I was successful, they celebrated with me, but they were quick to admonish me when I made mistakes. Lonnie's point was, "Boy, you need to slow down some. You can't do everything."

But I wanted to fix all the world's problems every single day.

My first budget week was in 2007. We'd usually leave by 8 p.m. on the first day of budget week. The second day we'd get out at about 10 p.m., and then the third day, to get it all finished, we'd stay at the statehouse overnight. We'd go through amendment after amendment and then vote on the extension of the budget. Back then, the budget was about $6–7 billion. South Carolina at the time also had an AIDS Drug Assistance Program (ADAP) waiting list. People on the list needed medications for HIV. South Carolina's list had 303 people on it, which was one of the longest in the country, but it would cost the state only about $6 million to get rid of the whole list and just give everybody what they needed.

The late Joe Neal was arguably the most compassionate member of the General Assembly. He represented lower Richland and drove every Sunday for an hour and a half to Chester to preach. He launched the effort to pay off the ADAP list, and I went up to the podium to argue his case with him because Bamberg County also had high incidences of HIV and AIDS. We were asking our Republican colleagues to vote for what was relatively just a little bit of money—less than one-tenth of 1 percent of the total budget. Yet vote after vote after vote was a "no."

One of my Republican colleagues stood up and said in a most pejorative way, and this is vivid in my mind, "If you make your bed, you should have to lie in it." I'll never forget that. I was so frustrated that I ripped up my amendment, yelled "We're killing people!," and then left the podium. I exited the building, went through the parking garage, and sat down in my office. I could still hear what was going on in the chamber from my office, but I needed to be by myself. I was so upset that there was so little compassion in that legislative body.

The African American House members, Lonnie, Seth, and Neal, were there to make sure I understood that the efforts we put forth were not wasted. We were chipping away at the glass ceiling. They told me I could not get frustrated at the lack of compassion in the hearts of other people; I just had to continue to speak for those who are voiceless. And lo and behold, they were right, because Kay Patterson, who served in the South Carolina State Senate and who wittily proclaimed himself to be chairman of the light-skinned Black Caucus, was able to get the money on the other side of the Senate to save those lives.

As the months passed and the presidential primaries grew near, I traveled around the country for Senator Obama, mostly to colleges and universities. I also took on the role as co-chair of his steering committee in South Carolina. Many of our elected officials still were not yet supporting him; they were instead supporting Hillary Clinton, and some, John Edwards.

Obama maintained a skeleton campaign staff in South Carolina. Besides Anton Gunn, only one other employee covered the entire state. Dick Harpootlian and I were appointed "committee members." Dick was the former chairman of South Carolina's Democratic Party and the shrewdest attorney I know. He has what we call "fuck it money," meaning he's a self-made man who doesn't have to answer to anyone any longer. *The Washington Post* once wrote a story about him headlined "Return of the King."

But Dick's also known for putting his foot in his mouth. Back in 1986, when he was running for a city council seat, he told a reporter, "I don't want to buy the black vote, I just want to rent it for a day." That quotation still comes up all the time, and I've always told Dick, who is a friend, that that comment was trash; but I also know Dick's actions speak louder than his words. I respect his political instincts, which are second to none. For instance, Dick was one of the first big names in South Carolina, white or black, to publicly say that Obama could win the presidency, which brought others into the fold.

Still, if Obama was going to win the South Carolina primary, we had to overcome two issues. The first was that black folk, especially older black folk, were afraid that someone would kill him. After all, we have seen so many of our leaders murdered. The second was that black people feared that white Americans weren't going to vote for Obama. They didn't know like we knew that the Obama campaign was basically a raw duplicate of Deval Patrick's successful campaign in Massachusetts several months earlier, when an amazing black candidate threaded the needle of his identity and weaved it to create a crossover appeal.

I called it casting your progressivism with a black idiom. You frame your progressivism through the lens of your own story. In other words, you don't forget who you are or where you came from. Deval framed his progressive views through the lens of his poor childhood, and Obama told his through the lens of Chicago's South Side.

Many people couldn't envision how the campaign would play out on a national level or how we'd get over those two hurdles. In fact, we never even crossed those hurdles before the South Carolina primary. The first one—the fear of assassination—was no joke, and we were woefully unprepared. In fact, the first time Obama came to South Carolina as a presidential candidate to speak, at the Columbia Convention Center, we had fifteen thousand people in that auditorium— with no security. One white state senator, who represents a large black constituency in Manning and Clarendon counties, later pulled me aside in the senate building and told me that would never happen again. He personally called the chief of the South Carolina Law Enforcement Division (SLED) and demanded that "this young man [Obama] gets security because he's not going to be killed on our watch in South Carolina."

Ultimately, Barack Obama did keep his word to me. Several months after receiving that call from him in April 2007, I got another one telling me that he was coming to my district and so I needed to help decide where we should have the event.

Michelle Obama had already visited Voorhees College. A hundred people showed up in Massachusetts Hall, right in the cul-de-sac of the college, which is a little more than a mile from my house. But there was no way we were going to fit Barack Obama in Denmark, or anywhere in Bamberg County, because we didn't have a place to put him other than in an open field. And we weren't planting Barack Obama in a field. So we settled on South Carolina State University in Orangeburg.

The day of the rally, January 22, 2008, I put on a suit and was feeling very confident. Way before we even pulled up on campus, I saw black people for miles and miles around. There were people from Maryland, Tennessee, North Carolina, and Virginia—it was the height of "Obama-mania." Everyone wanted to touch the metaphorical hem of Obama's garment.

I was surrounded by campus security and taken through the back door to the "green room," otherwise known as the men's basketball locker room, which smelled of socks and Gatorade. I walked in, and there was the comedian Chris Tucker and *Scandal* star Kerry Washington. Outside the room, I could hear the young crowd buzzing—well, it was more like pure ruckus. The Diana Ross version of "Ain't No Mountain High Enough" was turned way up.

Rick Wade, one of Obama's advisers, moved us upstairs to a little classroom where Chris Tucker, Kerry Washington, and I chatted. Then Wade peeked into the classroom and said, "I'm going to the Orangeburg County airport, I'll be right back."

I'd never heard of or seen anybody fly into Orangeburg County. I didn't even know we had a runway.

But then Wade returned with the superstar singer Usher.

Things were moving pretty slowly. Time was ticking. We were starting late because Senator Obama had to fly in as well. At that moment, it was just me with Usher, Chris Tucker, and Kerry Washington in that classroom. Usher's father had passed away about a week earlier. Although he didn't have a strong relationship with his father at the time, the death was weighing heavy on his heart. Tucker, with his famous high-pitched twang, kept us upbeat.

Usher looked at me and said, "You're the politician, man. I don't do these political stunts. What should I go out there and say?"

I was twenty-three years old and thought of myself as witty and clever, so I said, "Usher, man, just go out there and sing, and say 'Praise God!' and 'I love black women!'"

Soon enough we heard, "He's here. It's show time!"

Senator Obama glided in, shaking everybody's hand. "Y'all ready? Let's go! Let's do this!"

The energy in the gym was insane. I heard what seemed to me the voice of God announce my name first: "Welcome to the stage Representative Bakari Sellers."

I walked out onto near center court. All around the stage were steel barriers. People were screaming. The lights were blaring. There were people in all directions, so you had to talk while turning your body around to address everyone. There were international media representatives along the back wall. There were still people outside trying to get in, being placed, I was told, in overflow rooms. I had five minutes to say something useful.

I started by observing that the most important part of Martin Luther King Jr.'s "I Have a Dream" speech are the words "the fierce urgency of now."

I'm not a person who quotes Dr. King a lot because I think that his words have become sanitized and in many ways compromised. People want to hold King up not just as a martyr, but as some cotton-candy political figure. They've managed to strip him of his revolutionary identity. I will always view Martin Luther King Jr. as a militant negro who had a 37 percent approval rating and who was taken from us because of hate. It drives me crazy when someone asks, "What would Dr. King think today if he hadn't died?" That whitewashes what happened to him. He didn't die in his sleep or have a heart attack or a stroke. He was *assassinated*, which makes for a different question entirely. Dr. King was taken from us in the most violent way possible.

I hadn't really prepared my remarks for that day, but I had looked at King's speech. And I thought, "Man, we even have little black boys and girls in church that know the rhythm and cadence of 'I Have a Dream,' but nobody reads the rest of the speech." That's a shame because that entire speech is dope.

Not many people know that Dr. King had delivered versions of part of that speech earlier. The words "I have a dream" weren't even in the text that he planned to read that day during the March on Washington. But King was such a good pastor that at that moment, on the National Mall, on the steps on the Lincoln Memorial, he knew he wasn't taking the people to where they needed to be. Great speakers like King, and Barack Obama and many pastors in the South, *feel* when their audience is fully where they need to be. In my own way too, every time I give a speech, I want to move the audience someplace they were not when they sat down.

Back in 1963, it wasn't until the great gospel singer Mahalia Jackson hollered out to her good friend, "Tell them about the dream, Martin!" that his words soared into history. And Dr. King didn't just pull those words from his ass but from what he already knew. In June of that year, he had given a speech about "a dream" before 130,000 people at Detroit's Walk to Freedom. Indeed, now was "the time to make real the promises of democracy." He went out on a task-torial riff in Washington, DC.

So maybe that's why on stage, with Barack Obama in the wings, I felt Dr. King's words, "the fierce urgency of now," to be fitting. I was talking to young people in the audience, but I was also talking to some black folk from my district. I wasn't sure they knew how close we could be to having a black president and how urgent it was because all the polls had been saying that Hillary Clinton was going to steamroll us. For my purposes, I wanted people to understand we could create a ripple effect for the rest of the country to see.

Honestly, I didn't fully understand the magnitude of the moment I was in. When I turned around and introduced Chris Tucker, the crowd got louder. After five minutes, he introduced Kerry Washington. It was January and cold outside, but I was close to breaking out in a sweat because the lights were beaming down on us. Kerry Washington spoke and then introduced Usher. The women in the room swooned. It was pandemonium.

The first words that came out of Usher's mouth were, "You know, I want to first thank God and give a shout out to all the beautiful black women out there."

Usher, one of the biggest stars in the world, had taken my advice! We looked at each other and shared an inner chuckle.

By the time Obama walked out on the stage, the rails and bleachers were literally shaking. We were supposed to stand behind him while he spoke, at least those were the staging instructions. But people weren't focused. They were yelling out "Usher!" or "Chris!" or "Kerry!" There was too much star power on that stage.

The candidate noticed it, looked at us, and said, "Why don't y'all go to the back and come back out when I get done." But first he took a photo with all of us before we left the stage. "Come on," he said, "let's take this shot."

In that photo, Chris Tucker is to my left and the future forty-fourth president of the United States is to my right. To his right is Kerry Washington, and to her right is Usher Raymond, with his black power fist held high. Everybody was in the moment.

So many emotions were running through me when that picture was taken. Little did I know that it would go viral, that it would be published in *US Weekly* and still be a mural today at the South Carolina State Student Center.

When Barack Obama came out on stage that day, he said, "I have to thank Representative Bakari Sellers. He's been there for me from the start. He's an up-and-comer. He's being talked about not only here, but he's talked about around the country."

He gave me the biggest endorsement of my life.

Barack Obama won that South Carolina Democratic primary, but he also won the Iowa caucuses, which answered the second question black folk worried about: Would white people vote for him? It was a dream come true.

The black American poet Langston Hughes, in his famous poem "Harlem," posed an important question: "What happens to a dream deferred?" It becomes a "heavy load," or at other times perhaps "it explodes." If you're black in America you've recited that poem as a child. It inspired both Martin Luther King Jr. and Barack Obama. Its question "Does it dry up like a raisin in the sun?" inspired the play *A Raisin in the Sun*, which was named the best play of 1959. And it inspired me when I decided at a very young age to run for office, refusing to believe I couldn't help people in my hometown just because I was young. However, I believe that to make a dream come true, one must be organized and steadfast, like Dr. King and all those marchers and demonstrators. To be a successful leader, you must dream and envision the future but be practical enough to plan and strategize to make that future come true.

Being onstage with Barack Obama was a special moment because I was twenty-three and had fulfilled a dream. I was a leader. It was a dream I had started working on when I was seventeen, though I had been preparing for it since I was a little boy raised to have a purpose in life.

If I had waited to run for office, like some people told me to do, I wouldn't have been wrapping up my first term in the

South Carolina House of Representatives onstage with the future president of the United States. And it was all happening at South Carolina State University. I had gone to elementary and middle school at Felton Laboratory School, which was right across the street; for most of my life I had played in the gym I was now standing in. I was nineteen miles away from where I had told my parents that I was going to run for office. And I was three hundred yards away from where my father had been shot by white law enforcement officers during the Orangeburg Massacre.

VII

Risk Taking

The last time an African American was elected to a state-wide political office in South Carolina was back in 1876. Obviously, my state needed a change, which is why in 2014 I took a huge political risk: I decided to give up my seat in the state House of Representatives and run for lieutenant governor.

I was twenty-nine years old, and everybody asked me the same thing: Do you really think you can win? The answer was always—Yes!

I spent my twenties serving in the South Carolina General Assembly. I loved it, but I began to feel like I was growing stagnant. Running for statewide office gave me an opportunity to make history, and because of state constitutional changes, it would be the last time a candidate for lieutenant governor could run alone, on his or her own merits, rather than tied to a gubernatorial ticket.

But there was a deeper reason I wanted to run for that office. The roof of the cafeteria of Denmark-Olar Elementary School, which is just more than a mile from where I grew up, collapsed in 2010, without any news coverage, as if no one cared. The youngest of the school's students attend classes in trailers. When it rains, the children, all African American, trek through mud to get to their classrooms.

There's a reason why a collapsed school roof in the poor rural South received no press: because it's typical. On a statewide platform, I knew I could speak about the "Corridor of Shame," where thousands of rural children across the South attend schools that are dilapidated and falling apart. I'm a product of the proverb "it takes a village to raise a child," but all around me I was seeing the village crumbling.

And it wasn't just the schools; we had other issues that needed attention. Hospitals were still closed, especially in communities that needed them the most. People were traveling five hours a day for low-paying jobs, and the most vulnerable were drinking water unfit for human consumption.

Henry McMaster, my opponent, had been in political or appointed office since 1984. He had worked for President Ronald Reagan as his US attorney in South Carolina. He ran an unsuccessful bid for the Senate back in 1986 but ultimately became the state's Republican Party chairman and also the attorney general for the state. He was obviously a big deal, but we were a clear contrast. I believed I represented hope and the future, and he stood for the past.

One of the first things Jill Fletcher, my fundraiser, and I did was to visit Congressman Clyburn at his large district office at the intersection of Lady and Sumter streets in Columbia. I was excited to talk to the congressman about my ambition and wanted to get his support. Besides, he was one of the reasons I had entered politics in the first place.

At twenty-nine, I was still too young for some people, but I had a track record. I had built a school in Bamberg County and a library in Denmark, and I had brought a door company to my hometown. But there was so much more to do. We needed to fix South Carolina's schools, bring clean water to poor rural communities in the state, and help uproot politicians who were keeping our state stuck in the past. Unlike when I started to run my first election, I didn't feel the need to get support from local luminaries; I hoped I had earned their support by now. We were running to represent 4.6 million South Carolinians, not only the nearly 40,000 people I served in the House. This was a different type of race.

Still, I wanted Congressman Clyburn's support. When we met, though, he snickered and said, "If anybody could win statewide, don't you think I would have already done it?"

I was so taken aback that I actually gasped. The comment seemed rude, but I understood his point. For a very long time, my former employer had been a lone wolf, the only Democratic US congressman in South Carolina. He had had an unsuccessful run statewide, and so he understood the hardships any Democrat, and a black Democrat at that, was going to face.

Many people were not gung-ho and supportive. Like before, they thought I was too young and too inexperienced. But we didn't build the energy that surrounded the campaign by focusing top-down, or on political luminaries. Instead, we sparked excitement with millennials and people from ages eighteen to forty-five who didn't see me as young and inexperienced but seasoned and capable. We visited business leaders, church folk, and wide nets of influencers.

•   •

I chose Isaac "Ike" Williams Jr. as my campaign manager. He's also one of my closest friends: I often say we've known each other since before we were born because our fathers were in the civil rights movement together. Ike was my aide at the statehouse, charged with serving the day-to-day needs of my constituents. I was juggling law school, my legislative duties, and commuting between Denmark, Columbia, and Charlotte in North Carolina to see Ellen Rucker, my fiancée and future wife, so Ike was my liaison on many fronts. He was also a political consultant, with many successes under his belt. He had been the field director for the mayor of Columbia and later became Bernie Sanders's South Carolina political director.

But back in 2013, I asked him, "What do you think about me running for lieutenant governor?"

"If you think this is the right time to do it, I got your back," he replied.

We immediately talked strategy, we looked at dates, and Ike told me who we'd need to meet. Soft spoken and hardworking, Ike made the campaign run as smoothly as possible, keeping in contact with other campaign staff, checking mail and emails, driving me around, and making sure everything kept moving.

Jill Fletcher had raised $700,000, so besides Ike, I hired two Republican consultants—Republican because I wanted people who knew what it was like to win in South Carolina. We had a small paid staff but a large pool of volunteers. Ike and I named close to fifty team leaders, many of them from various colleges and some who were part of Young Democrats organizations.

Ike believed people were excited to see an energetic black Democrat make a serious run for a major statewide office. "People were impressed with how smart he was," Ike says, "and no one had seen someone this young step to the plate and be so articulate about policy." To this day, he says millennials, both black and white, never doubted I could win. Overall, we had about 250 volunteers fanned out across the state.

But among those who didn't get on board, most were shocked that I was serious about taking on McMaster. "For a young African American to not give up hope, people started thinking, well, maybe he could do this," Ike recalls.

For sixteen months, Ike and I traveled to forty-six counties. And then we did all those forty-six counties again during the last thirty days of the campaign.

• •

One of our first stops during our thirty-day tour was a church in Britton's Neck, which is in Marion County—one of the poorest areas in the state. Outside the church a man was frying a large pan of fish. Inside, the room was packed with mostly

African Americans. I try to meet people where they are. Everyone in that room reminded me of people in Denmark, people you'd bump into at the Piggly Wiggly.

"You know, I believe I have the audacity to look at people and say that it's not about black or white," I told them. "If you ain't got health insurance and you're white, and you ain't got health insurance and you're black, you know what? You're gonna get sick, and it's going to bankrupt your family. It's the same problem. I can't tell you what's going on in China, I ain't never been there. But I can tell you about what's going on in South Carolina right in Bamberg County. Let's say you break your toe. You know you gotta go thirty or forty-five minutes to the nearest hospital? Because the hospital sign in Bamberg County, you know what it says? 'In case of emergency dial 911,' because it closed in 2012. And what are we doing about it? Absolutely nothing."

Those last thirty days were grueling. A day would start with us talking early in the morning, and we'd hit the road by 8 a.m., driving from one end of the state to the other, sometimes through more than three counties a day.

• •

Ellen said she knew that it was going to take a lot out of me to run for statewide office. She understood it could be a long and sometimes ugly campaign, which it was. She also knew I was going to be away a lot, but she supported me because she understood this wasn't just something I wanted to do, but something I *needed* to do.

I met Ellen in 2008 at a wedding in Cancun. She's one of eight children; her late father was a dentist and her mother is a homemaker. She grew up in Lancaster, South Carolina, within a very tight-knit and religious family. Her sister Ruby introduced us. I was immediately attracted to Ellen, who my sister claims fit what she said was my type: gorgeous, country, witty, and grounded.

A hair product entrepreneur, Ellen is only five-foot-three, which my six-foot-two sister Nosizwe jokingly says she doesn't understand because all the women in our family are so tall (our mother is nearly six feet tall).

"The day that he met Ellen, he called me, and he said that she was beautiful, but when I got to know her, I saw she's beautiful on the inside too," Nosizwe said.

Ellen was eight years my senior and divorced when we met, but that didn't matter to me. She also had a three-year-old daughter, Kai, with her ex-husband, the NBA basketball star Vince Carter. Although Ellen and I didn't interact much during that Cancun trip, I told Kai while we were all in the swimming pool, including nearby Ellen, who was within earshot, "I'm going to be your dad one day." Rightfully and hilariously, Kai said, "I already have a daddy," and swam away. To be sure, I've never again told anyone I'm Kai's dad (though she is my daughter), but mainly because she has an amazing dad. I'm a bonus dad. I know my role.

During that "courting" period in my life, I was wrapping up my first term as a legislator and gearing up for reelection. I was also twenty-three years old and broke. Most people do not realize this, but South Carolina legislators make only $10,000 a year, plus reimbursements. I had just finished law school but was so busy that I couldn't prepare adequately to pass the bar exam. I secured a job at Strom Law Firm, where I still work, but at the time I wasn't yet a licensed lawyer, and I also owed $113,000 in school loans.

Still, when we returned to South Carolina from Cancun, I sent Ellen flowers and asked her whether I could take her out to dinner. With all of eighty-three dollars in my pocket, I drove up to Charlotte to see her. She lived in a beautiful high-end condo near the SouthPark Mall. She picked a nice wine bar that served tapas, but little did I know Ellen likes lamb chops, which are expensive. Now, when you don't have a lot of money, and you're dating above your means, you best allow your date to order first. Your appetite, or should I say your budget, ought to be based upon what she orders. If she orders a lot, then you're just not hungry. The bill came to seventy-six dollars, and so I skated by.

It must have been a great date, because we've been talking ever since.

By the time I was running for lieutenant governor, Ellen and I were planning to marry and have babies. However, the campaign kept me on the road all the time. "He's from one city to the next," Ellen told a documentary filmmaker, who was following me throughout the campaign. "I don't see him. It's just like any other long-distance couple. . . . You know, we text, we FaceTime, we talk on the phone every morning, every night."

I would be lying if I said it wasn't difficult to be away from
Ellen and Kai for an entire week, but they supported me to the
very end of this journey.

· ·

There are many reasons why neither African Americans nor
Democrats can win statewide elections in South Carolina: Although African Americans make up more than 60 percent of
registered Democratic voters, the party doesn't engage them
during midterm elections or coordinate efforts to get out the
vote—and my race was in a midterm election year. By the time
each of these election days come around, according to most
polling data, African Americans often are disillusioned and
stay home.

So I asked my consultants, "How many white voters do I
need to win statewide if I maxed out African Americans?" One
said that South Carolina Democrats typically can count on
one of five white voters. That's about 18 percent, the other
consultant added. Accordingly, we were hoping for a race
where I would max out black voters and increase white voters
from 25 to 35 percent. That was our strategy.

Obama's South Carolina primary win informed us and convinced me that we could make history. We also counted on a
good debate, and we already realized the campaign generated
lots of media. Poll numbers were slowly growing.

The problem, that second consultant explained, was that
the trend for white people in South Carolina was to vote less
and less for Democrats.

"So, what do we do?" I asked. "Stop focusing on black people?"

No, she said—start focusing on whites.

She was right, but it was easier said than done. I would have been more comfortable trying to max out the black vote, which was potentially huge in South Carolina. I believed we could build a Democratic base by increasing African American turnout. Some days I felt like we were getting closer, other days, not so much.

About two weeks before the election, on November 4, 2014, I had a meet-and-greet in a cozy home in Darlington. Most of the people who attended were retired African Americans. I said to them that in our beautiful state, "We do two things very poorly. We hold onto old ghosts . . . whether it's the Confederate flag or anything else. And we just send the same folk back to do the same thing, and we don't get any different results."

An older gentleman spoke up. "I think historically, we just haven't found that the off-presidential election years were that important."

I shook my head. "Two hundred and sixty thousand African Americans who look like me and you showed up for Barack Obama. Y'all cried all those tears the night he won and thought we'd overcome something. But then we didn't come out in 2010. Every single vote in these off-year elections matters—they all matter. It's not often we say this in an election, but we have a chance here to make history in South Carolina. It's amazing that we have that type of power. We have to have that same type of energy now."

"We believe in you," the man said. "You're an extension of our dreams. I'm eighty years old. My wife is seventy-nine. There are so many things we want to see for our children and grandchildren, and you represent hope for us. You don't know how excited we are about you."

Although it was encouraging to talk to black voters, who believed they had a stake in my winning, I stayed the course we charted: I tried hard to increase the white vote, which was often an uphill battle in South Carolina. It's such a red state that people will tell you to your face that you'll never win because you're a Democrat. We stood on street corners with signs, and people were just mean. They ignored us or spit out hate not only about me, but about the Democratic Party and, of course, then–President Obama.

Others were kind as could be and supportive. Some older white American voters would come up to me and give me the biggest hug and kiss and say, "I've never voted for a Democrat, but I'll vote for you." Young white voters would tell me, "I encouraged my grandparents to vote for you."

These kind words kept me going through the tough times. And there were many.

Ghosts and Trolls

Here's a sample of the hateful tweets I get every day: "Pussy nigger, just because I proved you wrong on Twitter you blocked. That does not make you powerful, it makes you a chicken shit nigger." Or, "I like blacks, but I hate niggers. You, my friend, are one of those niggers and an ugly ass chimp in a suit."

The hate came in the form of tweets, letters, and phone calls. Ike recalls I got hundreds, if not a thousand, tweets and hate mail during my eight years as a member of the South Carolina General Assembly. My run for lieutenant governor generated lots of buzz and news coverage, which Ike believes also energized the hate. I laughed off most of the comments because that kind of hate speech was far too common for me to waste my energy getting upset about it. Besides, most comments were just racist, not threatening, though a few times I had to involve law enforcement.

· ·

I challenged Henry McMaster to renounce his membership at a reportedly all-white country club. I told MSNBC: "I just want Mr. McMaster to join me in thinking about ideas to move forward. And yes, I challenged him to renounce his membership because I want people to be able to look at South Carolina and see that we're raising the stature of our state, that we no longer have to be held back by those ghosts of yesterday."

McMaster was part of the problem, part of a culture in South Carolina that refused to change, part of the culture I needed to root out. McMaster, whose good ol' boy ways had done him just fine, coolly told the news organization through his campaign manager that he didn't plan on resigning at a club where he'd been a member for more than three decades.

It's been like this forever in South Carolina, but my dad always said it doesn't have to be this way. He'd reassure me, if not provoke a little bit: "It'll all change with your generation, but you still have to pick up the mantle and go ahead and fight for it."

I was wary. "I'm not sure when that will happen."

Yet, despite all those people telling me I was too young, my father knew it was the young people who make the change: Martin Luther King Jr. wasn't even forty when he was murdered. "You have to take those risks and put yourself in those kinds of positions," he said. "That's what it takes to come in as a young upstart and run a campaign and be successful."

What was left unsaid was the fact that others would make damn sure to try to stop me from doing just that.

• •

Two years before, on October 7, 2012, I had been pulled over by a Chester County sheriff, who asked me whether I had been drinking. I had, but I wasn't drunk. I was returning from a University of South Carolina–Georgia football game while likely driving too fast along I-77, just after 1 a.m.

And so, during my run for lieutenant governor, a video of me being arrested became public. I was anxious that it would go public, but I wasn't shocked when it did. The case eventually was dropped because the evidence didn't add up, but I still pleaded guilty to reckless driving. I was too sleepy to be driving that night, and so I exercised bad judgment that grew into something that will be with me forever.

One of the most off-putting things about running for the statewide spot was that a Republican tracker was sent out to follow me. Everywhere we went, a tracker was there—usually the same medium-height, stocky white guy pointing a video camera at me during speeches. Sometimes he'd hide in bushes, but he nearly always showed up at our meetings, hoping to catch me drinking or doing something I wasn't supposed to do. Or he would just give McMaster's people information on what I was saying. It made me extremely nervous and anxiety-ridden to have someone pointing a camera at me and stalking the campaign. Sometimes our volunteers would try to shoo him away, but most of the time we ignored him.

The Church Fish Fry

I am aware, of course, of the role the black church played in the civil rights movement, but I have been disappointed with the church lately. During the past fifty years, the church has retreated from its rightful spot as a bastion of activism and is losing its definition. Once the epicenter of change, black churches in some cases have been transformed into hollowed-out megachurches, where pastors are thirsting more for fame than social justice.

However, we are starting to see the emergence of a new generation of social activists who are also pastors and faith leaders, whether it's Jamal Bryant and his fight to prevent unjust police shootings; or William Barber on the front lines of transforming the political landscape of North Carolina; or Sarah Jakes Roberts, William Murphy, and Charles Jenkins, all using their ministries to teach members of their flocks to be part of something bigger than themselves.

And still, we have done some backsliding. Since Dr. King's death, the church has become passive and insular at best at a time when it needs to be younger and more progressive. For instance, it must become more active. In my father's generation, activists used church buses to shuttle people to vote and church buildings to hold community meetings, and pastors were never afraid to speak their minds on issues that affected the entire community, not just members of their own churches.

Today, and this is purely a political observation, in American society, the GOP is seen as "God's Only Party." Just as "the working-class vote" in the media often means the white vote, as if other voters don't work, "the Christian vote" often means the Republican vote. But what reporters don't seem to realize, or maybe are overlooking, is that African Americans are conservative in their religious beliefs.

Despite my challenge to the church, I have spent a lot of time there, either to feed my own spiritual life or to build community; and so I know that if you want to move black people to the ballot box, you have to move them spiritually and you have to move them in their places of worship.

Therefore, if you want to run a political race in South Carolina, it's essential that you visit as many churches as possible. The African Methodist Episcopal Church, in particular, is one of the most politically persuasive bodies for Democratic politics in the region. What the Southern Baptist Convention is for white folk, the AME church is for us. I went to all of the churches during my campaign, and I knew church protocol from my experience running for the statehouse: You call a week before your visit. You see the pastor first, and then you say your piece to the church parishioners. My maternal grandfather was a Baptist minister in Memphis, and he always said, "Make sure when speaking at a church that you leave the preaching to the pastor."

Political fish fries at churches are often how to meet hundreds of potential voters. They are never held in the main sanctuary but in the fellowship hall, which all look alike: a spacious room in the back of the church or in the basement. The floor is always tiled, bulletin boards are hung on the walls, and the kitchen has that little cutout window through which members can be seen cooking up grits and fried fish. It never fails that the walls are adorned with a framed portrait of Martin Luther King Jr. and Jesus. And as the years passed, President Obama's photograph was added to the mix.

In these churches, the ministers are second in importance to the church ladies, who organize voters, make sure the church-run buses are ready on Election Day, and help people fill out absentee ballots. These ladies often, but not always, are also the ones cooking the fish. The churches almost always serve whiting because it's cheap. Whiting is also delicious after it's been fried golden in hot grease and Lawry's Seasoned Salt and slathered with hot sauce and mustard. You walk into the fellowship hall to the sound of crackling and popping and the smell of hot grease wafting through the air. Every politician knows you eat white bread with fried fish, but they're also aware that white bread sticks to your teeth and the roof of your mouth like glue. If you're an elected official, the thing you don't want to do is get that white bread stuck in your teeth. So you need to use your tongue and suck that bread off your teeth very, very hard.

A country biscuit might come with your meal, but if you're at a real country church, you'll likely be served some liver pudding with the fish and grits.

My Great Friend Clem

Near the end of the race for lieutenant governor, I attended a fish fry meet-and-greet with Vincent Sheheen at St. James AME church in Walterboro. Vincent was the Democratic candidate for governor. Although we were not running together, in a way we were running mates.

Ike and I rode to the church together on a Saturday morning. The Reverend Clementa "Clem" Pinckney greeted us as we pulled up to the church. Clem was both a longtime South Carolina state senator but also the pastor of Emanuel AME church in Charleston. One of the oldest black churches in the Deep South, it is known as Mother Emanuel. This particular day, Clem was at St. James as one of the luminaries.

I was feeling bruised and weary, and Clem seemed to notice. He walked toward me, and in his deep "Barry White" voice, he asked, "How are you doing?"

"I'm tired," I said. I was at the end of the road, the end of a tough campaign. Clem must have seen the stress, because he said something I will never forget: "Bakari, just keep going, going, and going."

He was adamant that I not be tired, that I not flirt with quitting. He needed me to continue on. It was like he was admonishing me for saying I was worn out because we just couldn't afford for me or anyone else to give up. There was so much more to do, so many more battles to be fought.

He looked hard at me. "Leaders like us, we have to keep going," he said. "Bakari, we're praying for you."

He was always uplifting, but that day he was almost insisting I stay strong because it wasn't going to get any easier. When Clem was elected to the statehouse, he was the youngest member of the State Senate. Our districts also overlapped. He took me under his wing because of our young ages, but Clem, who was forty-one at the time of my run, was farther along in his spiritual journey. He had become a preacher at age eighteen and a member of the South Carolina House of Representatives at twenty-three—not much older than me when I had been elected. He was supporting my run for lieutenant governor for a specific purpose: because I wanted to expand Medicaid. I think that if we could have done that, Clem would have just walked away from his political duties as a member of the South Carolina Senate and focused solely on the church.

About fifty Colleton County voters showed up as we were

served fish and grits. I love fried fish, but after sixteen months of it, I honestly had had enough. Often, there's a deacon over at these church meet-and-greets. This time it was a young woman named Kay Hightower, who was what we called a "faith connect" or "plug." Her job was valuable to politicians because she coordinated the faith community's outreach with campaigns.

As I looked around the hall, I realized we had lost Clem. "Let me go find him," Kay said. Although we were in a church, Vincent Sheheen and I were dressed casually in jeans, loafers, church socks, a pressed shirt. Clem, however, always wore a full suit, so he was easy for Kay to find.

Clem introduced us and said of Vincent, "He will lead our state to a new place." Then I told the crowd I was on a journey similar to David when he faced Goliath. "There are a lot of people who say I can't win because I'm young, who say I can't win because I'm black, or who say I can't win because I'm a Democrat. And then there are those who say I can't win because I'm a young black Democrat. But I want you to vote for me because of what we believe in, and that's a better South Carolina."

I asked everyone to embolden friends and relatives and co-workers to vote, including every high school senior at Colleton County High School.

• •

Near the end of the campaign, we were running on fumes. Ike and I were both so tired that we sometimes forgot to eat, despite all the food around us.

One of our last stops was at an event with a business organization. It was different from my other stops, but Ike and I
thought it was important to try to engage them. The crowd
was nearly all white, and they seemed attentive, if not cautious.

It was obvious that my energy was not high as I began my
speech about healthy foods for kids and in Bamberg County,
getting to the point where I say, "I tell people often that growing up in a small country town like I did, there was nothing
more important than being able to spend time with your family around your meals on Fridays. . . ."

And then I stopped talking. "I'm not feeling well," I said,
as several men rushed from the audience and got me seated. I
couldn't remember if I had eaten the day before.

I caught my breath and said into the microphone in a weak
voice: "I'm sorry, but I'm Bakari Sellers. Give me a shot November fourth for lieutenant governor . . . if I'm still around."

Ike led me out of the hall. "How about some orange juice or
something?" he asked. "You feel like your sugar level's down?

• •

Lancaster County was the last stop on our South Carolina tour.
"We are exactly twenty-four hours away from the possibility of
making history," I told a crowd. "And we're tired, we're worn
thin. This journey has been long, it's been arduous, it's been
tough, people write you off, newspapers write you off, polls write
you off. But polls don't vote. We do. We have so much power.
And tomorrow we have an amazing opportunity to prove them
wrong." I pointed to a black child in the audience. "We're not

running for anything else other than for this little girl in this yellow shirt right here. So that she can dream big dreams."

My voice began to quaver, and tears swelled in my eyes. "So, my name is Bakari Sellers and tomorrow, seven o'clock," I said, holding up the mike, and then my voice shook, "Victory!"

Ellen ran toward me, "Baby, you did so well!"

Election Night—November 4, 2014

Election Day was sunny. I had a skip in my stride and a win, I felt, under my belt. I had requested a debate for months, but McMaster continually evaded me. I had started tweeting every day he didn't respond, and finally, at around Day Seventy, he agreed. At our one debate, he had spoken about the past, about working for Ronald Reagan, and he tried hard to link me to Obama, but it was clear I had won our match. Voters on the streets stopped me and applauded. The media and others dapped me for a particular jab about McMaster's years on the government's dole. "You've been receiving so many government benefits over your career, there are some welfare queens out there who are probably jealous," I said.

When I had questioned his ability to create jobs, McMaster claimed, with a smile, that he had created a bunch of jobs by putting people in prison. I came back at him, exclaiming that there are no jobs in prison.

I was convinced we were going to win; we were going to make history. I felt a calm come over me and was excited as I brought a box of Krispy Kreme donuts that morning for the volunteers, as I always do for my precinct on Election Day. I laughed a bit with some of the volunteers whom I see every election year, handed the donuts to one of them, and then voted. "All right, ladies. Y'all don't let her eat all those donuts," I said as I walked out the door.

Election Day was all calm, but Election Night was intense.

All of us—Ellen, Ike, the consultants, and others—sat in front of the computer screen in the Hilton Presidential Suite in Columbia. Lionell, one of our campaign staff members, clicked on the computer as I verbally navigated him.

It started off good: Bamberg County was on fire. "Alright, there we go, 1 percent in. Alright, we're keeping pace. Go back to my feed," I said. "Oh, what is that? Whoa, whoa, whoa! What'd you just . . . what'd you just pop up?

"We got Fairfield," someone said.

"Ahh, alright. Take a picture! What is that? That's what I'm talking about! One down. Forty-five more to go. Oh, Sun City's in? Look at that. We're okay!"

But then suddenly we weren't okay.

"You're only down eight thousand votes," Ellen tried to reassure me.

"Fourteen thousand," I muttered. "Shit . . . Do we have any more precincts out? Let me see . . . is the city of Anderson in?"

I shook my head in despair. "My goodness gracious."

Soon enough, it was over. I got 41 percent of the vote to McMaster's 59. McMaster won 75 percent of the white vote and 10 percent of the black vote.

During an emotional concession speech, I told my supporters, "I'm not going anywhere. . . . The absolute reason that
they're going to have to deal with Bakari Sellers is because I
love South Carolina." I broke down; the tears would not stop.
"Thank you and God bless you all."

Some reporters were kind that night. One television anchor
said, "An emotional Bakari Sellers, is, of course, a rising star in
the Democratic Party, so I have to agree, we probably haven't
seen the last of him any time soon."

I knew I was going to win that race and make history—up
until I didn't.

I questioned myself: Did we raise enough money? Did we
do a good enough job getting people out to vote? But we knew
exactly what the problem was: there just weren't enough votes
out there for a Democrat to win.

Ike believed I was so impressive to people I met around
the state that if I had been a young white man, I would have
won the race. But I don't think that's true. It would have been
closer, certainly, but win? Probably not. I'm still a Democrat
in South Carolina.

Looking back, it was a victory for me and others like me:
the fact that a young, black Democrat, in the deepest of red
states, could earn 41 percent of the vote was promising, if
not downright incredible. Many in the political world were
shocked. For us, it meant things were changing, and one day
it will be possible for someone black or Democratic to win a
statewide position in South Carolina.

I always tell people that we chipped away at the glass. In

South Carolina, in 2014, I won 41 percent of the vote; in Georgia, in 2018, Stacey Abrams won almost 49 percent; and in Florida, in 2018, Andrew Gillum secured 49 percent.

So, here's a trend for political consultants: we're getting closer.

VIII

Anxiety

A Black Man's Superpower

I inked my first tattoo during the beginning of my junior year at Morehouse. It's a portrait of my father across my chest. I have two crosses tattooed on the back of my arm, and I have angel wings on each rib; inside each wing is the name of my mother and my sister. On the right side of my chest, I have a portrait of a young black man reaching over a wall grasping for the hands of his brothers, entitled, "He ain't heavy, he's my brother." That tat is dedicated to Lumumba.

I have the names of my nieces and nephews inked on my right bicep. I have a famous Einstein quotation tatted inside my left bicep, which says, "Only a life lived for others is a life worthwhile." I have the word "Blessed" stretched across my back, from shoulder to shoulder.

My stepdaughter Kai's name is inked on my left arm and

my wife's initials on my ring finger. The tree of life is drawn on my left-arm sleeve. I whisper to my two infants all the time that I love them and their names will soon be on my body.

I suffer from anxiety, and all these tattoos keep my loved ones in my orbit every day, assuring me of their love and letting them know I love them.

I vividly remember the hot summer evening when anxiety took hold of me and never released its grip. It was June 1996, and I was eleven years old, riding my bike when my mother called me to come inside the house. It was nearly dark, but she was beckoning me because I had a telephone call. My friend Crystal was on the line. Her father coached basketball in middle school, and her mother was a nurse. We attended the same elementary school, Felton Laboratory, on the campus of South Carolina State College.

I heard her voice on the other end of the line saying, "I called to let you know Al died."

Everything went quiet, except for a silent inner scream: Al is dead!

Our friend Alfred McClenan was called Al. He was a year ahead of me in school, an upcoming ninth grader at Orangeburg-Wilkinson High School. Al and I hooped together in middle school—we were not best friends, but his death changed my life.

Thirteen-year-old Al collapsed during summer workouts for B-team football. I later heard that he had complained of pain in his lower left torso and then fell over. He asked to remain there on the field until his mother came to get him. He was still conscious when she arrived, but then he passed out. He didn't wake up after that. The newspaper said Al had had a heart attack.

I began to visualize, as kids often do, what occurred during the moments of Al's death. Was he hot or cold? Was it like going to sleep? Did it happen quickly, like in the movies? Did Al's memories, his hearing, the feeling in his hands and toes and heart, just melt away? He would never attend college. He wouldn't get to play football again. He wouldn't graduate from high school. He'd never get married.

These thoughts triggered in me a profound fear of death. Most young people have a sense of invincibility or immortality, but anytime something puts a dent in that at an early age, it can cause problems.

I know that's what happened to me.

My mother drove me to the memorial service at Orangeburg-Wilkinson, where eventually I attended high school. We pulled up to the school after the service had started, so I stood in the back of the auditorium. Mom didn't come in with me but let me enter near the end of the service. I now think she was being cautious because this was my first experience with death, and it was a peer's death—a child's death.

Al's older sister gave a very upbeat speech at the memorial. In the black, rural South, we don't have funerals, but home-going celebrations of life. I remember his sister saying when he was first born and brought home from the hospital, he looked like a "cute little frog."

At the end of the ceremony, I walked down the sloped aisle

to the front, where I looked into his casket. That image of a thirteen-year-old boy, with his lips pursed, as happens when a body is embalmed, is still seared into my mind.

Unraveling the Source of My Anxiety

After Al's death, it was a very tough summer. At night, I felt like I was dying. I could barely breathe, my chest hurt, I was having anxiety attacks that felt like a big knot sitting on my chest. This happened every night. Sometimes I cried, many times I got up, and often I didn't sleep through the night. In fact, that summer I mostly slept during the day: I'd play basketball and then come home to lie down, often beside my mom, who struggled with her own anxiety issues.

My parents sent me to physicians because by now we could afford that, and I was subjected to a full medical workup. I took a stress test, where you run on a machine with oxygen, and found out I had a heart murmur, but that wasn't the cause of my problems. Next, my parents took me to a psychological therapist, who prescribed medication. I was probably one of the youngest people I've known on the antidepressant Wellbutrin.

The adults were trying to check my emotions, but later in life I realized that my issues were likely hereditary. Al's death might have triggered the anxiety, but I probably got it from both parents. I'm almost sure my father suffers from anxiety that he doesn't even know about, and I believe it's linked to his losing so much during the civil rights era. So many of his friends were cut down; he's seen so much violence, experienced so much hate. Then there are the ghosts and scars from the Orangeburg Massacre and the fact that some people still blame him for the violence. I tell people my dad's eyes don't pop like they used to because of shedding so many tears, and his shoulders aren't as upright as they once were from carrying the burdens of so many generations. I think my anxiety also may be connected to the Orangeburg Massacre, the event that has shaped who I am as much as it shaped my father.

My mother suffers from immobilizing panic attacks. Her hands shake, and sometimes all she wants to do is sleep. When I was a child, she spent many hours and days in bed. She says it's much more than a sense of being overwhelmed: "It's scary for a person like me," she tells me, "because I am a control freak. In the midst of a panic attack, I don't feel as though I have control. What I do is withdraw until I feel that I have control."

Maybe I shouldn't have been surprised to discover that my mother believes her anxiety is also triggered by the trauma she experienced when my father was sent to prison several years after their marriage. She never used to express this to any of us, but now it all makes sense. My parents fled South Carolina and went to Greensboro, North Carolina, before my dad's imprisonment because his parents worried about his safety. During those years, my mother was living in an unfamiliar city with a newborn baby (my sister Nosizwe). Her husband was locked up for allegedly instigating a riot, during which three people had been killed, and the governor of South Carolina blamed him for everything.

She called her parents for help, but she says they didn't sympathize with her situation. She wasn't sure what to do but survived by relying on her own instincts. And yet, according to my mother, she was surely in the throes of an anxiety attack but didn't realize it.

"I did not handle very well Cleve's pending incarceration, and the ramifications following that," she now reveals. "I did not live a life that equipped me to imagine prison as being a reality for people. I was clueless. I bore our child while he was in prison. . . . I went through the pregnancy, and was raising the child, and then figured out how we were going to go back and forth to Columbia and visit Cleve in prison. I think what saved me was Nosizwe—no matter what happened, I had to take care of her."

My mother's ability to cope, despite the hardships, is a testament to so many black women and the strength they show. But the anxiety that caught hold of my family, I now suspect, is also a testament to how the struggle for equal rights has left us all with everlasting scars. The Orangeburg Massacre left my family with a father burdened by a felony charge, a mother raising a baby without the man she loved, and a baby girl born without her father. Of course all of this pressure produced anxiety; how could it not?

Nosizwe, who had toxic arguments with my mother through the years, always says Daddy was a brilliant and loving father, the best father in the world, but he probably didn't know how to be the greatest husband. "Daddy would circumvent Mom," Nosizwe says. "I thought why he did it was probably right, but I do realize that a lot of the issues that she had with their relationship are very valid. And a lot of the things that he did probably made it worse."

My mother's anxiety came with mood swings, which meant she could be the salt-of-the-earth-damn-near-first-lady-of-the-church mother in the morning and then the harshest, most mean-spirited . . . words escape me to describe how disruptive she could be in the evening. And then the next few days she couldn't get out of bed.

But don't for one moment think I am saying her mental health made her weak, because that would be wrong. She survived, becoming the breadwinner during those periods when my father's felony record made it hard for him to make a living.

Still, we can't pretend that mental health issues are merely "life ain't been no box of chocolates." It's more like life is a snake pit, and, while in it, you don't know whether you're going to find a garden snake or get bit by a water moccasin. It's that tough.

After my parents took me to a therapist to investigate the cause of my anxiety and headaches, my oversleeping and then not sleeping, a theory emerged, through a process of elimination, that indeed I was afraid of death. I refused to go to funerals, and after they prodded me, I'm sure I talked about Al's death.

By myself, I linked a lot of the issues I was having to my mother. My relationship with her became particularly fragile around high school. I was going through eighth, ninth, and tenth grades, excelling academically and socially. Even in college, I was coming into my own politically and maturing and having healthy relationships with everyone but my mother—which is kind of different compared with most black men.

My mother and I were very close when I was young. I was close to both my parents. Since my dad was always working late, though, my mom and I used to travel together to conventions she attended. She read to me, we played games together, she taught us children how to speak properly without using "um." But around when I was in high school, my mom stopped cooking. I often say that she hasn't really cooked since the Chicago Bulls broke up, which was in 1998; since then, my dad has done all the cooking. Her behavior changed. I didn't understand how to handle it, and I don't think I was strong enough to handle it, so in response, I became very distant from her. By the time I was in law school, I went months without talking to her because I didn't know what I was going to get in return.

These days, my mother is doing better through talking to people and taking medication. And even more important, she recognizes that she has a mental health challenge. Very strong people, very independent people often don't believe that they have such an illness. They don't believe that they're affecting other people the way that they are. My mom may have taken a while to get there, but at least she's there now. And I think that's the challenge for all of us who struggle with anxiety and related difficulties.

My own anxiety, which in part expresses itself as a fear of death, is linked to the work I feel I still have left to do. Meeting that ultimate moment petrifies me because of all the things I still want to accomplish. Truth be told, even before Al died, I heard a lot about death. During every Orangeburg Massacre anniversary, I listened attentively to families discuss the pain of having lost a relative and all the details of how they were killed. All of that was branded on my brain. My mother never liked me to attend those anniversaries. All that talk of killings and sorrow, she believed, was no good for a child. She'd see my father crying onstage and then turn to see my little face wet with tears as well as I sat in the audience watching my dad. "Just boohoo-ing," she recalls.

My father is my hero, and he has passed his torch to me, but could the weight of that responsibility also be the source of my anxiety?

The Weight of the Torch

I fear death, but I also fear failure, which I see as a sort of small death. When you're black and from the South, failure affects more than you. For those of us who have been fortunate enough to escape or leave the proverbial traps and have a platform to affect others, failure is not just letting ourselves down, but letting down our parents, our communities, the church ladies. I am letting down those people I'm carrying the torch for—those who wanted to go to college but couldn't, and those

ancestors who died, all those people who bled, sweated, and
toiled. Failure for a black man from the South is costly. When
you fail, you're failing not only the Emmett Tills of the past,
but also the Michael Browns of today.

I know my truth, and I know right from wrong. But every
misstep I make—even when I was pulled over by the Chester County sheriff and accused of drunk driving—are hard
moments because I feel like I let so many people down. At
that time, facing the sheriff, although I did not do what I was
accused of, I put myself in a bad situation where I could be
judged. That driving arrest was a secret for four months. I
couldn't sleep. I couldn't eat. My anxiety ran high. And when
the story came out, I had to deal with it straightforwardly in
public.

Social and political pressures can make it hard for me to
breathe, but this is my normal now: I go out and try to make
sure that other people can breathe by revealing my own fears
and anxieties. Regardless of how hard it gets for me, I've been
blessed, and I'm fortunate, because I have the means and the
support to help me cope with the stress. But I also know many
people do not.

• •

When you get elected to public office, you want to be great,
you want to be legendary, you want to be remembered for
changing people's lives, for destroying systems of oppression,
for being a public servant, not just a politician—but all of that
comes with a price.

Since age twenty, I've lived in a fishbowl, where everybody gets to see every facet of my life. When I go out to restaurants, people are watching me, eavesdropping on private conversations. The media may report on where I went, what I said, what I did—and I'm like, "Wait a minute, I didn't do that." The only profession that is like politics is the ministry because people expect more of their ministers than they expect of themselves.

Young people often tell me they want to go into politics. I then ask them whether they have ever heard of someone being half pregnant. The answer is always "no." Then I explain that it's the same with politics: you can't do it halfway. You're either going to be in politics or you're not. It's all-consuming, and there will be many ups and many downs. I tell them, you'll wake up or go to bed at night with knots in your stomach because you won't know what the next day will entail; what the next news article, online comment, or tweet will say; what the next polls will hold. I tell young people, you just have to run fast; you're running against your opponent, you're running for so many people who have been left behind, and—guess what?—you're trying to outrun your fears as well. Sometimes it gets exhausting, sometimes you'll cry and break down, but that fear, that rage and anger, can be forged and transformed into motivation: that's how you become successful. At least, that's how I became the youngest state legislator and later a commentator for CNN.

I try to be open about the pressures that come with being on television, particularly being one of only a few black newspeople on national television. I try to be humble, in part because the way people see me on television is the way they will see a lot of young black people, particularly young black males. I can't have an off day. I can't go into the lights and not do well today because then that's the way people—yes, many white folks in this country—will look at young black men on the street tomorrow.

I remember a piece of advice my father gave me: never argue with a fool because the people who are watching can't tell the difference. So when I'm on television, I know I can't change a person's mind. I just try to talk to my audience.

A few years ago, I had an interesting conversation with the radio and television personality Charlamagne Tha God. A product of Moncks Corner, South Carolina, Charlamagne went from selling drugs to attending night school to becoming one of the most controversial and influential radio hosts in the country. Presidential candidates are sure to want to talk to him. Charlamagne is also a great friend of mine who has been open about his own anxiety and has even written a book about the subject. During our conversation one day on the set of his radio show *The Breakfast Club*, we discussed how prevalent anxiety is among African Americans and in our own families. "I remember my mom taking nerve pills," he said. He talked about his own panic attacks, saying, "It feels like you are going to die."

I told him I could talk to him about politics in Israel, the environment, and tax policies, but when it comes to my anxiety, I stutter because for so long I saw mental health challenges as a form of weakness. I think many black men still do. To this day, for instance, I do not think my father understands my anxiety.

For many black males, anxiety is grounded in a sense of self-directed anger and rage because our lives appear to be cyclical—to borrow from the rapper T.I., we find ourselves in a proverbial trap. From attending failing schools, to suffering from poor health, to seeing our loved ones gunned down, we feel like we can never get out of this trap.

Some of the anger and frustration comes from black men not being told they are loved—they are not loved by society or the media—and they are portrayed as savages and thugs. The only people who really love us are black women.

Many of my brothers have a difficult time expressing this shared frustration, because they feel they can't show deep weakness. Black men are not expected to verbalize, outside of barbershops and locker rooms, that we might need some help. Our own somewhat self-inflicted distortions of manhood, which come from carrying so large a burden—one that is centuries old—projects as an unwillingness to show weakness. And, of course, this often means that our emotions simmer. For some, that leads to bad decisions. I have peers who suffer from the same things I do, but they mask that suffering with women and alcohol.

Black men with platforms like Charlamagne and myself can use our anger, which is expressed as anxiety, in the same way superheroes use their power, as a force for good. A popular saying goes, "Pressure busts pipes, but pressure makes diamonds." We can use that rage to be woke in this country and understand the systems of oppression around us in order to rebuild our communities. Rebuilding a white community and a black community are two totally different things. Because black folk were stripped of everything, we have to rebuild our communities mentally, physically, spiritually, and economically. So the most powerful thing we can do, and the way I live my life, is to be an example.

There's that 2009 photograph of a sharply dressed five-year-old named Jacob Philadelphia, standing in the Oval Office while President Obama leans down so Jacob can touch his hair. Jacob had wanted to know whether he and Obama had the same haircut. That image is the most powerful image Obama sent to the black community, because it taught little brown people around the globe that they too can be the leader of the free world. When we lead by example, we make the soil more fertile for the generations to come.

Yes, I want to set high expectations. Right now, in our community, we have a culture of low expectations; the bad thing about this is you get what you expect. And so, I make sure when I'm back in these communities, in the poor rural South or in urban Los Angeles, that I try to be an example of excellence.

Researchers say my generation as a whole, regardless of race or gender, is the most anguished in history. We're certainly at least the most medicated. Like no other generation before us, millennials are afraid of death and failure. We've seen our friends die in senseless wars; we've watched the world we were just getting to know change before our eyes after September 11, 2001. We've seen the world get meaner and colder. We've seen black men shot over and over on the streets by people who are supposed to protect them. We've seen women now naming their traumatic experiences, speaking truth to power and pushing back on a culture that has persecuted them and manipulated their bodies.

Back in 2003, three young men from Orangeburg died in the Afghanistan war. One of them, Darius Jennings, a high school friend of mine, was killed six months after being deployed. A shoulder-launch missile toppled the helicopter carrying him and about thirty other people as they flew over a hot spot in Fallujah. Elaine Johnson, his mother, has been a staunch supporter of mine, but I can hear the pain in her voice as she carries her son's banner loud and proud. She never talked about him in the past tense until recently, spending twelve days in Fallujah. I think about how she ushered her son out of the poor, rural South, imagining his bright future. So, I live for Darius.

We are a generation that feels the pain of having to live for all those who left so early. When I graduated from college, I was doing it for Darius and for so many others, and when I got married, I got married for them, too. All of the life moments that I am now experiencing, I am also experiencing for them.

Suffering from anxiety has never stopped me from performing because that anxiety is rooted in a fear of not being good enough, so I always want to do better. People can give a great speech or run an awesome political race but still suffer from deep anxiety. Like when I was younger, I have many moments in my life when I cannot sleep. On many days, I just worry.

Sometimes I feel like I want to throw up in the morning, or I gag but there's nothing there. I'm hot, I'm sweaty, and I'm consumed; my mind is racing a million miles an hour. I'm worried about what's going to happen next.

But then I ask myself: What am I afraid of? And then comes courage, the one thing no one ever regrets.

Turning Anxiety to Strength

My mother says the reason I'm angrier about what happened in February 1968 than my father, to whom it all happened, is because I view the Orangeburg Massacre as the thing that hurt my father—my hero. There is some truth to this. But the pressure I feel about what happened is not just the pressure of living for those innocent young black men who died during the massacre, before I was born, but for those who've died during my own lifetime.

After I lost the race for lieutenant governor, I was a little bit wayward, because I had given my all. And one of the things that I did early in the race, which was very risky, was announce that I was going to resign from the House of Representatives. I didn't have to, and I could have run for both offices at the same time, but I wanted people to believe that I was all in. I was going to be the first black official elected statewide since

Reconstruction. I wanted people to believe that I was going to give them everything. I did that, and I got beat.

And then the terrible summer of 2015 approached.

Every single thing I stood for, and everything I was raised to do—living for those who could not and continuing the work that my father and all my "uncles" and "aunts" started during the civil rights era—were put to the test. I had to face my fears of death and failure in the most tragic ways. But those fears and anxieties motivated me to do what I was raised to do: to speak for those who cannot speak, to be the living example they have not had the chance to be, to stand our ground.

IX

A Voice for the Voiceless

Anger and Anxiety

We're politically spoiled in South Carolina because we're home to the first southern primary, which means we get to meet all of the presidential candidates right out of the gate. On the night of June 17, 2015, I attended a fundraiser in Charleston for Hillary Clinton. The event was hosted by celebrity lawyer Akim Anastopoulo and his wife Constance, right on the water where the ships come in on East Bay. The house was beautiful, and naturally I admired their full basketball court. Every big state Democrat was there. I talked to former governor Jim Hodges and Mayor Steve Benjamin of Columbia. Jill Fletcher, my fundraiser, and her mother Candy accompanied me. Of course, we were all there to see Hillary.

At the conclusion of the event, sometime close to 9 p.m., I

asked Mayor Benjamin and his driver, a Columbia police officer, whether Ike could follow behind his car. As we made our way back onto Meeting Street, which turns into I-26, we noticed something strange. Emergency units, police cars, and other law enforcement vehicles were blazing by us in the opposite direction—a blur of unending lights, sirens, and police cars that seemed to go on for miles. Then I found something shocking on Twitter: "Nine people dead in Charleston church."

I needed to find out what was happening. I called to check on Jill and Candy, who had left earlier for dinner at Hall's Chophouse. "Are y'all alright?" I asked them.

"We're okay," Jill said. "But the city seems to be on lockdown."

Then I received a devastating call from Tyler Jones, a friend and member of the South Carolina Democratic Caucus. "There's been a shooting at Mother Emanuel, and Clem's been shot," he said. The last time I had seen Mother Emanuel's senior pastor had been at the fish and grits meet-and-greet about seven months before with Vincent Sheheen during his run for lieutenant governor.

I started making more phone calls and found out that nine people definitely had been shot at Mother Emanuel and many were dead, but I couldn't discover specifically who was dead. I reached Kelvin Washington, the US marshal, and I talked to state Attorney General Alan Wilson; I believe they were keeping me up-to-date because there was the potential that as a major candidate for a statewide office, I might be called on to comment.

Soon enough, to our horror, we learned that nine African Americans had been killed by a twenty-one-year-old white supremacist named Dylann Roof. When he had walked into Mother Emanuel earlier that night, he'd been warmly welcomed to join the Bible study. In fact, he asked for Clem and sat next to him. After nearly an hour, when everyone closed their eyes for benediction, he started firing a .45-caliber Glock pistol. He shot Clem first, and he shot many others, even pumping eleven rounds into an eighty-seven-year-old woman. After nearly everyone was injured or dead in the room, the shooter kept firing rounds.

That Wednesday night, we didn't know any of this yet. Neither did we know that Clem's wife Jennifer had been in the pastor's office with their five-year-old daughter and was probably still cowering there when I first saw the emergency crews rushing by. In the coming days, we learned from her cousin that Jennifer heard the shots and hid with the child under a desk. "Don't say anything," she demanded of her daughter, placing her hands over her child's mouth.

Then we started to hear whispers of a survivor. We later learned that the killer walked up to Polly Sheppard, a retired nurse, and asked, "Did I shoot you yet?" When Polly told him "no," he said he was going to keep her alive to tell the story.

But as the evening of June 17th grew darker, the story was still an unraveling mystery. And as crazy as this might sound now, we didn't know at first whether it was a hate crime. Everyone was still trying to process what was going on. In part, I think, we were in shock. The national media, already in town for Hillary Clinton and for the Republican presidential candidates who were coming to the state, were clamoring for reports and, like everyone else, for answers. The city had no time to adjust, and so we were suffocated by a tsunami of national press.

Malcolm Graham, a former North Carolina senator and a self-professed news junkie, told me he was watching MSNBC when he saw the ticker scroll across his screen at about 9:30 p.m. His family had been attending Emanuel AME Church for six decades. A native of Charleston, Malcolm now lived in Charlotte, but he often visited the church where he and his five siblings grew up singing in the choir and attending Sunday School in its basement—where the killings had just happened. His sister Cynthia Graham Hurd was very much a current part of the church family.

"Automatically I got the phone and called Cynthia," he told me. "Although I've lived in Charlotte, she was my link to all things Charleston. I called her to find out what the hell was going on down there, and no one answered the phone. And so I said to myself, well, you know Cynthia, she's right in the middle of everything trying to figure that out, trying to know herself, and she will call me back. But an hour went by and she didn't call."

That disturbed him, because she'd normally call in any emergency to say she was okay. Several hours later, their niece called to say no one could find "Aunt Cynthia" and that she believed Cynthia had been attending Bible study. At that point, Malcolm knew in his gut that she was at the church and somehow involved. And he did not want to find out bad news from the media. Helpfully, he had a friend who was the chief of police in Charlotte. "He got word to me that from those who were able to leave the church, they identified Cynthia as being at the church. Before it was publicly known, before even my family knew, I knew from talking to the chief of police in Charlotte that my sister had been identified as being one of those individuals who was shot. It was just heartbreaking."

Stories like this were happening all over as family members were hearing from survivors or trying to figure out whether a loved one had made it out alive. Many were learning of the horror from the news. While Ike took me home, I got a call from Jerome Heyward—a social activist who's like a big brother to me. He was weeping: "I can't believe someone shot up Mother Emanuel! I can't believe they shot up the Mother!"

My tears started flowing the moment I got out of the car and stood in our driveway. I called my two most important mentors: Pete Strom, the founder of the law firm for which I worked, and, of course, my father. Pete had already gone to bed by the time I reached him, so his wife asked me whether it was an emergency. I might have been able to get the words out, "They shot Clem in a church." She woke Pete right away, and like everyone else that night, they switched on the news. Knowing how close I was to Clem and how emotional I naturally am, Pete comforted me and kept telling me that somehow everything was going to be okay.

My father also coolly guided me. Even without knowing

what had happened, he knew that Clem had been gunned down for no reason and explained I had to prepare for what I needed to do—which was to think clearly, to try to stitch together the pieces of what had happened, and to speak for those who couldn't speak for themselves.

When I walked into the house, I hugged Ellen, and we wept together.

I told her I had to return to Charleston the next day. I didn't know what I was going to do, but I felt I had to be there. I got through an emotional interview that night with WIS-TV in Columbia and then poured some Jameson in a cup and went to bed with the heaviest heart. I woke up, packed my bag, and ended up staying in Charleston for two weeks.

· ·

The media trucks that Thursday were choking the entire block from the church on the corner of Meeting and Calhoun streets. The television crews had set up white tents where they stationed themselves and their gear. I wondered whether they understood the irony of what had just happened here on Calhoun Street. John C. Calhoun, the namesake for the street running by Mother Emanuel's steps, had been a nineteenth-century vice president under John Quincy Adams and Andrew Jackson and an unrepentant slave owner who vigorously defended slavery—which is why he was nicknamed "John C. kill a coon."

Other roads leading to the beautiful white church were filled with flowers left by strangers. Gorgeous makeshift vigils popped up in front of the church. People of all colors came to the neighborhood to pay their respects to the dead.

I stood near the media tents with Todd Rutherford, who's also African American and is South Carolina's House Minority Leader. Photos of Columbia, our state capital, were all over the news channels. Flags were flying half-staff—except for the Confederate flag. We were, like—what? We called Patrick Dennis, the chief legal counsel for the South Carolina House Judiciary Committee at the time. "You know that can't come down," he said. "That's a state law."

To her credit, then–Governor Nikki Haley, whose parents are Indian American Sikh, wanted the flag down, but she couldn't do it alone. There needed to be a vote of two-thirds of state legislators to remove it from the statehouse grounds.

At around this time, pictures began to emerge of Dylann Roof enveloping himself in the Confederate flag. We began to highlight this fact during television interviews. Something else made us stop in our tracks: Father's Day was dawning on us, and Clem's two little girls would not be making brunch for their father. That hit me hard, so much so that when I mentioned it during an interview with Al Jazeera America, I broke down. "I know this has been a long day," the commentator said, thrown off by my sudden inability to speak. I couldn't stop the tears. All I could think about was Clem's daughters.

The reporter and the viewers could see adults and children laying flowers on shrines behind me, which obviously prompted him to ask next, "What do we tell the children?"

I sucked in my breath. "I'm not sure I know the answer to that today," I said, and then added: "What we can tell them is that we can do better, we must do better, and we will do better."

This was supposed to be a small, quick interview, but of all the interviews I did during those two weeks, this one went viral and was seen all over the world.

People referred to those killed as "The Emanuel Nine," but in South Carolina we knew there were so many more people destroyed by the shooting. Take Malcolm's family. Of six children, fifty-four-year-old Cynthia was the fourth and the oldest girl. Aside from her five siblings, she also had nieces and nephews and other close relatives, all of them mourning her loss. She was a librarian with the Charleston County Library for thirty-one years and worked part time for sixteen years at another regional library. She had built years of relationships with her co-workers and was so much a part of the community that two days after the killings, an emergency Charleston County council meeting was held, with only one agenda: rename the library where she worked after her. It is now called the Cynthia Graham Hurd/St. Andrews Regional Library.

Malcolm's family had been part of Mother Emanuel for six decades; his parents were buried in the church's cemetery, as would be Cynthia. Her life touched hundreds, if not thousands, of people. Now, multiply that loss by nine.

Malcolm found the media to be so intrusive that he was compelled to make a relatively quick decision. The night when

he discovered Cynthia had been one of the nine killed, he resolved to stand up and tell her story and explain her positions
and beliefs. "Here's a lady who had so much grace and dignity,
was killed in the fetal position underneath a table," he told me.
"I decided that she deserved to have a voice, that she would not
be remembered as just being a victim."

Not diminishing the fact that nine people died together,
Malcolm still believed his sister was an individual, and she had
her own hopes, dreams, aspirations, and way of thinking that
he wanted her to be remembered by. "I felt comfort in the fact
that she did not die alone. If that makes sense. But she also was
this tremendous, impactful individual, that deserved to stand
on her own merits as an individual."

. .

As we stood outside Mother Emanuel, some of us compared
the tragedy to the Boston marathon attack, after which Massachusetts governor Deval Patrick, rightfully so, put the city
on a voluntary lockdown when one of the perpetrators was
still on the run. This made us all wonder why Charleston
mayor Joe Riley and chief of police Greg Mullen hadn't done
the same. But in the end, we came to realize and appreciate
the infinite wisdom these South Carolina public servants indeed had.

The morning after the shooting, police released video of
Dylann Roof entering Mother Emanuel. Everything from his
bowl haircut to his gray sweatshirt to the black car he drove
were clearly visible. The video was everywhere on television

and shared across social media platforms. And it wasn't more than twenty-four hours after the shooting that US Marshal Kelvin Washington drove to the church, rolled down his car window, and shouted to me and Todd, "We got him!"

Earlier that day, a florist in Shelby, North Carolina, about four hours from Charleston and very close to Charlotte, noticed a young man driving a little black car just like the one that had been broadcast. She took down his license plate number and called police.

Todd and I repeated out to the crowd what Washington had just told us. It was an insane feeling. The atmosphere outside the church was tense, but a sense of jubilation bubbles up when people come together to celebrate lives but also to unite in fighting wrongdoing.

Hailed as a hero, the florist, Debbie Dills, would not accept the label. "It wasn't me," she told *The Today Show*. "It was God. He used me as a vessel."

Speaking Truth to Power

Undoubtedly, like my dad, who wanted to live for Emmett Till, I wanted to live for and give voice to Clem and the other victims of this horrific crime. In Charleston, I too became a vessel, pushing forward only because I was hopeful tomorrow could be better.

During the early days of the tragedy, CNN anchor Kate Bolduan interviewed me, asking some tough questions. She was polite and gracious, but it was an example of a dance that all of us had to do, careful not to say anything that would distress the families of the victims while still speaking truth to power. Kate's first questions were why Dylann Roof intentionally picked these people and why this historic church.

Where do we start to even try to answer that first question? Why have black people been subjected to a torrent of violence right from the time the first African set foot on these shores? Today it is Mother Emanuel, but in 1963 it was the bombing of the Sixteenth Street Baptist Church in Birmingham where four little girls were killed. In 1968, it was the Orangeburg Massacre. Sadly, even more comparable to my father's Emmett Till generation is the symptom of overzealous cops and those organized to defend the unjustified killings of people of color. Like those white-helmeted officers in Orangeburg, Dylann Roof saw the nine people he killed in the church as being less than human. We'd heard rumors; friends and relatives of Roof told the media that he believed in segregation, believed African-American men were raping white women and that black people were taking over the world.

Kate's question why this church got me thinking. Whenever you're able to inflict pain on the black church, you got to the heart of who we are. It cuts at our core. That's why they bombed the Sixteenth Street Baptist Church in Alabama and likely why Dylann Roof walked into Mother Emanuel.

Still, why did he choose Mother Emanuel? Established in 1816, Emanuel is the oldest AME church in the Deep South and has one of the oldest black congregations south of Baltimore. The church was cofounded by Denmark Vesey, a literate former slave I always admired and who had planned a large slave revolt. When white landowners found out about Vesey's plans, they burned the church building to the ground. After Vesey's capture and hanging in 1822, Vesey's son rebuilt the church.

There's a 2013 video of Clem speaking about the history of the church to a mostly white group of visitors. Though only in his late thirties at the time, he has the elegance and demeanor of a much older man. His deep baritone voice is pitch perfect, calm and loving, as he says, "It's a very special place, because this church—and this site, this area—has been tied to the history and life of African Americans since about the early 1800s."

When he politely asks the group to bow their heads in prayer, it's a heartbreaking moment to watch because I now know bowing his head in benediction was the last thing he did.

The church was always a force for social change. Booker T. Washington and Martin Luther King Jr. spoke at the Mother. It's also part of the powerful African Methodist Episcopal organization. To give you a sense of the AME's reach, think of this: if I were governor of South Carolina and Clem's dream of being AME bishop had come true, he would have been more influential than me in the South.

I didn't want to evade Kate's questioning; however, it seemed that every hour we were learning of a new twist or turn to the story. Also, people were just so tired—many of us hadn't slept, and others were still in disbelief. So her question was important, very damn important, but at that moment, it wasn't at the top of my priority list. I pointed out something that was troubling, but also a testament to how fresh our wounds were. Right behind where I was standing was the church parking lot. And the cars of the people who had been killed the night before were still parked there.

I decided to answer Kate's question. "I think this gentleman was filled with hate," I told her. I also explained I could not understand how someone who's only twenty-one years old, born in the nineties, could have the same mindset and outlook of racists of the fifties and sixties. "We need to figure out the answers to 'why,'" I said. "But right now, we are hugging, caring, loving, and praying."

Governor Nikki Haley believed Roof should get the death penalty, and Kate wanted to know my opinion about that. It was a tough question for a politician to answer. Truth is, I have a serious problem with the death penalty, and I told her so. It disproportionately affects African Americans. As a lawyer, I said, I am quite aware that witnesses lie and sometimes DNA evidence is discovered decades later that exonerates someone. But if there were ever an individual who deserved the death penalty, I said it would be Roof, who walked in the doors of Mother Emanuel filled with evil.

Kate asked whether I'd seen Jennifer, Clem's wife. I told her I had not because I was giving her space. But when the cameras are gone, I said, we will still be here for Jennifer and all of the grieving families.

Anger Is Not a Sin

I was on nearly every television news station—except Fox News. I had no interest or time to allow a Fox News anchor to browbeat me for my beliefs on what racism is and what I consider racist. I was being asked by the media to speak for the church victims, for their families, and to try to answer what this all meant. I was angry, and I was sad, and I did not have all the answers, but I was going to put my best foot forward for those who couldn't speak for themselves.

As I kept thinking about the question of "why us," I realized that deep down I knew the answer. It's simply because of the color of our skin. This has been the answer for four hundred years. The related question is, Why does dark skin so offend white people? There's no value in skin color itself. It adds nothing to or detracts from a person's skills, heart, or humanity, any more than eye or hair color does. So why have people with dark skin been terrorized for centuries, to this very day, and held in such contempt? Why were we enslaved for 250 years? Why were so many public initiatives to support former slaves, going back to Reconstruction, half-baked? Some say because of fear, hatred, or even jealousy, but does the "why" really matter? Considering what we've been through, how much we've been oppressed, for how many centuries, it's remarkable that we continue to fight and we are still strong. What we've been through has caused us anxiety, great stress, but we've turned that pain into strength. I said all this to whoever listened.

For instance, Black Lives Matter asked me to speak at a

march and rally they organized in Charleston. There was concern about our safety, so we decided to have the march in broad daylight. I recalled what my father always warned, "People do things under the cover of darkness they would otherwise not do."

My speech was brief, but I knew that I wanted it to have some rhythmic cadence and be something that people could *feel*. I quoted a gospel song, but mostly the words came fast and furious, flowing straight from my heart. "I want everybody to know that this terrorist did not win. He wanted to invoke terror and fear. But we aren't for that. We are standing up together, arm in arm, or on our knees, with our faces to the rising sun, praying to our Lord and telling him that we will not bow down, but we will stand up."

Sometimes you are thrust in a moment. During some interviews I wasn't "television ready" but soaking with sweat from the Charleston sun; sometimes my sadness and anxiety kicked in. But I kept going because my people, our people, needed a voice—which brings me back to Malcolm Graham.

No one needed to speak for Malcolm. The media sought him out not only because he was the brother of one of the victims, but because he was an articulate former politician, someone who spoke the truth. After the tragedy, Malcolm and I talked many times, usually after a panel we were both on. We talked about our anger and we talked about our frustration.

"What made me even angrier," he told me, "was not that my loss or someone else's loss was any greater, but it was other family members who said two days after the shooting that they forgave this killer. I was just beyond angry that here it is two days after this guy did the most hideous thing in the world, that they forgave this man."

He understood the media, and therefore he knew that the "forgiveness" sound bite would be transported nationally and across the globe, and people would confuse forgiving the killer with a community coming together, celebrating the lives that were lost and understanding humanity.

He also knew that "turning the other cheek" had a religious element to our older generations. Malcolm understood that families had a right to that response, but it offended him. Recalling conversations he had with his sister about race and justice and discrimination, he says, "Cynthia would have been like 'No, hell no. We can't forgive this right here. We got to prosecute this thing. Because what happened at that church was not only a crime against those who were there and those who were killed, that was a crime against a race of people, a crime against humanity and a crime against the Christian church. Those things just cannot be forgiven.'"

Malcolm and I made a connection because he knew I also used my voice to continue telling my father's tragic story and that of the victims of the Orangeburg Massacre. He knew I understood his point. Malcolm believed he came across sometimes in the moment as an angry black man, but, he says, "Bakari was able to articulate it in such a way that when I saw him on television talking about the incident, then and now, I say 'Yeah that's what I meant. That was my point.'"

He believed I understood the complexity of the situation

he was struggling with, the anger that bubbled up. And I did understand why he was angry, but I didn't have any better of a hold on my anger than he did.

I always tell people that President Obama may have had the dreams of his father, but I inherited the anger of mine. And if anyone had earned the right to be angry, I'd always thought, it was certainly my dad. Anytime I got angry as a child, or even as an adult, I would call my father to vent—and he always reminded me that anger, even when justified, is not enough.

It's never a substitute for a plan.

• •

My father and I did an interview outside Mother Emanuel with Melissa Harris-Perry for CNN. "I'm thirty and my father is seventy," I said. "We shouldn't be sharing the same experiences, burying our loved ones. It's traumatic and has to change. We must redirect history."

The shootings traumatized me and angered me, which I think was reflected in my interviews with Al Jazeera America and with Melissa Harris-Perry. I was angry about the situation, angry about where we were, and angry that someone took Clem from his family. The tragedy made me realize that when someone asks about how far black people have come, politically and socially, the answer is, Not fucking far enough— we're not where we need to be. We are very far away from any mountain top. That doesn't mean that my dad's work in the 1960s was in vain, but that the ground plowed then was probably harder than anyone imagined.

Ten days after the shooting at Mother Emanuel, I was interviewed by Martha Raddatz, who was that day hosting ABC's *This Week*. I sat outside in front of the church with South Carolina state representative Carl Anderson and Martha. The conversation quickly moved to the Confederate flag.

"Our good friend Clementa Pinckney is going to be lying in state in the rotunda of the state capitol thirty yards away from the Confederate flag as it will fly high and wave in the slightest hint of wind," I said. "And that banner, that flag, it may not have killed Clementa, but it gave his shooter and others like him a banner under which to justify their actions. And for me, that's maybe even worse."

After the interview, I got a cup of coffee, and then I got a private call from CNN asking whether I'd do commentary on race and legal issues for the rest of the year. Humbled, I knew I had an opportunity to fulfill my purpose in life, to be a voice for my community. I am a politician and lawyer, but I became a commentator that day. I began to do hits on the issues I care about, during all times of the day and night, sometimes with Anderson Cooper, Chris Cuomo, and Alisyn Camerota.

CNN's international stage allowed me to give Clem's words power and to present his vision and speak for him and for so many others. An example of that is when I got tapped to be anchor buddies with Don Lemon on the day the Confederate flag came down in South Carolina. We were positioned right where it would be removed from the statehouse grounds.

People always get taken aback when I say it was an act of political courage by then–Governor Haley, who led the effort to take down that flag. And it was her efforts, along with activists like Bree Newsome, that the General Assembly, after a passionate debate, voted to do the right thing and remove the flag from the statehouse grounds. But the real truth is, the day before the Charleston massacre, you would have been a fool to believe that the Confederate flag was ever going to come down. It took nine deaths to remove that flag, but the governor and the rest of my colleagues did the right thing, though others put their heads in the sand. For one, Henry McMaster, my opponent for lieutenant governor, was nowhere to be found.

On the day the flag was to come down, July 10, 2015, people of all races started to converge on the statehouse grounds in Columbia that morning. By 9:30 a.m., thousands of people packed the streets for a ceremony that would take only minutes. I felt proud as I looked over to see my former colleagues, all legislators, line up with their families on the statehouse steps. I appreciated the candid remarks of Senator Larry Martin and Senator Tom Davis, who said they only recently had come to understand how offensive the flag was to so many people.

At 10:08 a.m., state Highway Patrol troopers began lowering the flag, and the large crowd burst with applause and cheers of "USA!"

When the flag came down, Don Lemon and I were right there, just twenty-five yards away. We shed a tear and high fived. Adding a little humor to this serious moment, I quoted the great American poet and rapper Flo Rida: "It's going down for real."

I saw the removal of that flag clearly as a moment of civil

rights triumph. It wasn't quite like my dad sitting in a chair near Dr. King and LBJ after the Civil Rights Act of 1964 was signed, but it was still historical. I felt like I could breathe again.

Hate took away nine lives at Mother Emanuel Church but transformed a community and a state. However, it's infuriating to think that we still have so many issues to deal with in South Carolina. People want me to say the flag is down and so we made it, but from educational woes, to lack of clean water, to women dying at the hands of their domestic abusers, I have much more work to do to change the political culture of South Carolina—because we are not there yet.

X

Why Are the Strongest Women in the World Dying?

For black folk, here is our burden. We have to love our neighbors even when they don't love us, which is such a difficult weight to carry. When we live under these systems of oppression, watching injustices infiltrate our communities, knowing our people are being put upon, spat upon, degraded, we still have to fight back, but we must love those individuals who are part of this system of oppression. You must do it, even when they don't love you. That is why we cling to our religion because we must have some sense of hope. I think that if we were to substitute that love for hate, then it would simply eat away at us. We would never survive as a group.

If carrying this burden of not being loved by your neighbors requires strong arms, no one carries the weight like black women.

First, let's define strength. When I try to break down what a strong woman looks like, I think of my great aunt Jennie Marie Sellers, the matriarch of our family. Born in the early part of the twentieth century, she was an educator at Voorhees College, trained in the Booker T. Washington school of philosophy and instructed in the idea of elevating self through hard work, farming, and craft. She taught men how to use their hands to make a living and women how to be dieticians and caretakers.

Resourceful and a brilliant cook, she used the "goober," a boiled peanut and an African culinary staple, in everything from cheesecakes to oyster soup. In South Carolina, if something is unbelievably delicious, we say, "So good you wanna slap you mamma." Her mamma-slapping sweet potato and her coconut pies were always seductively waiting on the window ledges, so that the waft of nutmeg and vanilla hit you before you even walked in the door.

Aunt Jennie always sat in the front row at church. She dressed to the nines, wearing a big hat and enough perfume that when you hugged her you would smell like Chanel the rest of the day. She was fiercely independent, still driving a car in her late eighties and early nineties. I remember my father having to go over to her home and have "the talk" with her, the talk that should have happened many years earlier because she wasn't able to see after dark and was bumping into everything.

When I think of my aunts Jennie and Florence (the Aunt Florence who taught me how to shave), I think of dignity, pride, and self-care. They were never afraid to watch over you, whether it was saying a prayer in church or holding you when you cried. My father often observed that in the civil rights movement, for him, it was Emmett Till's mother who was the change maker, the brave one, showing the world what bigotry and hate looked like with the open casket that held the brutalized body of her son.

My father was very conscious in teaching me about strong individuals who may not get all of the notoriety but who are the backbone of a movement. The women in the civil rights movement were the ones making things happen. For instance, activists had to go through a women's board at a church if they wanted to persuade a (male) minister to galvanize the masses.

Fannie Lou Hamer, a middle-aged sharecropper from Mississippi, didn't look like the brilliant strategist that she was. Although she was severely beaten with other activists while traveling through Mississippi in 1963, she remained a thorn in the side of the power structure. In fact, her widely broadcast speech at the 1964 Democratic National Convention in Atlantic City scared President Lyndon Johnson so much that he interrupted it. His actions only raised her profile as a major powerbroker in the fight for voters' and women's rights.

There would not be a Hillary Clinton or a Barack Obama if it were not for the bravery of Congresswoman Shirley Chisholm, who ran for president in 1972 under the slogan "Unbought and Unbossed." Yet during that run she watched women and old-line black Americans abandon her because they never believed she could succeed.

I think about such women, these treasures in our lives, our North Stars. They are the strength of our communities; they feed you when you need sustenance, and they hold you when you cry. God knows I cry enough.

. .

As I write this, I think about my own sister, who recently stayed with me and kept me strong as my wife Ellen was near death shortly after our twins were born. I think about how months earlier Ellen, determined to have our babies, calmly prepared me for hard times that surely would come.

The Harlem Renaissance writer Zora Neale Hurston famously described black women as "the mules of the world." Speaking through her character Janie Crawford, the protagonist in her classic 1937 novel *Their Eyes Were Watching God*, Hurston was not insulting black women by any means but planting a kiss on the collective foreheads of her fellow sisters. The mule is "worked tuh death" and "had his disposition ruint wid mistreatment" and yet was able to carry immeasurable loads—like the black woman.

Black women never had true allies. White women sacrificed and fought hard in the civil rights movement too, but they were just a handful. Black women have also fought against the oppression of black men, but where are the black men in the fight for black women?

After fifty-some odd years, the country is finally starting to understand that African American women dictate the possibilities of who our elected officials are or who they can be. What we witnessed in 2016 is that more than 95 percent of black women voted for Hillary Clinton, who could have been the first female president, but 53 percent of white women voted for Donald Trump, someone who clearly doesn't stand for women's rights. I don't have the audacity to know why that is; in fact, I wouldn't dare make assumptions. But I will say that black women always vote in their own interests where other groups may not. They hold people accountable, whereas other groups do not. They are the reason we achieved civil rights, and the reason we were able to elect Barack Obama.

Black women help put white men in office too, like Alabama's Doug Jones, but the favor is rarely reciprocated.

The Benefit of Their Humanity

Despite the importance of these women, no one seems to care about their health concerns. We have lofty conversations about Medicare for All, universal health care, and the Affordable Care Act, but nobody is ensuring that black women have access to physicians who understand them.

The maternal morbidity rate in the United States has been rising. According to a 2015 editorial from the World Health Organization, between 1990 and 2013 that rate more than doubled, moving from twelve to twenty-eight maternal deaths per one hundred thousand births. And according to the Centers for Disease Control and Prevention, black women are three to four times more likely than white women to die of pregnancy- or delivery-related complications in this country.

There could be many reasons why black mothers are dying

at such high rates in the most powerful country in the world, such as previous lack of medical care and poverty for some. But what can't always be explained is why black women with access to good health care are still dying at higher rates from pregnancy- and childbirth-related difficulties. In fact, per the CDC, college-educated black women are more likely to die during childbirth or pregnancy than non-college-educated women of any other race. Could obesity be a factor? Black women who are an "average" size are more likely to die during childbirth or while pregnant than women of other races who are obese. What about the communities they live in? Could that be a factor? But black women living in the wealthiest communities are more likely to die in childbirth than poor women of any other race. So, what's going on?

Growing research is showing that doctors don't perceive a black woman's pain the same as a white woman's pain. In too many cases, a black woman's pregnancy complications are just not completely addressed.

In February 2019, Virginia governor Ralph Northam resisted resigning his position after a 1984 yearbook photo allegedly showed him wearing blackface and standing next to a person in a Ku Klux Klan robe. A day after admitting the photo was of him, he denied it and then said, oddly, that he had worn black face to imitate Michael Jackson. What was especially traumatizing for me and many African Americans is that Northam is a physician, and the photograph appeared in his medical school yearbook.

Jake Tapper at CNN asked me to be part of a panel to discuss all of this. I said we need to set a standard whereby racism is not tolerated, but I thought people were missing the point. Northam is a medical doctor. "We talk about systemic racism all the time," I said, "but the fact that you have doctors dressed up in black face—how do you think they are caring for African Americans in their care when they do not even look at African Americans or give them the benefit of their humanity? This is why racism is pervasive and why we have disparities in health care. This is a larger issue than Governor Northam."

Sadie and Stokely

January 7, 2019. My wife, Ellen, is on the edge of death.

Postpartum bleeding is the number one reason why women across the world die during and after childbirth. And it's the reason why Ellen was hanging on for dear life after giving birth to our twins.

We arrived at the hospital at 3 p.m. Our son Stokely, of course named after my "uncle" Stokely Carmichael, was born at 5:28 p.m. Sadie was born at 5:32 p.m.

By 11:15 p.m., Ellen was nonresponsive.

I was handed two tiny babies while my wife was dying. It was just me and the babies for three hours.

That day started off busy and exciting, but there was a feeling of anxiety in the air. Still, everything had been planned to perfection. We knew the genders of the babies, we had their names picked out, but a few things still made us nervous. Our daughter would be named Sadie, after Ellen's great aunt who never had grandchildren. Ellen and I were very well aware of the high mortality rate of pregnant black women, regardless of socioeconomic status, which led Ellen to switch her OB/GYN team to a group of black female physicians who looked like her and would understand and respect her concerns.

Despite all the preparation, nothing went as designed. We sent text messages that everyone coming to see the babies should get flu shots, though Ellen's large loving family didn't all follow through. My sister, who has two small children, called to tell me my father was pacing back and forth in her house. He wanted to come down and have a talk with us before the birth. We were not going to deny him that, but we had errands to run, things to do. Ellen wanted to have her lashes done, a ritual for most women I know. I needed to go to the gym. Kai, my thirteen-year-old stepdaughter, was at school.

I called my sister Nosizwe to ensure she'd be in the room with us when Ellen went under anesthesia (she was scheduled to have a C-section), but she didn't have the heart to tell me that she didn't have the authority to be in the delivery room with us just because she was a doctor. She'd be sitting in the lobby like everyone else.

However, after how everything turned out, she wondered whether I had sensed something that no one else had.

• •

Ellen wanted to have a vaginal birth, but God was telling us that the babies were not supposed to come out that way. She had a fibroid, which is not uncommon among women, especially black women. Fibroids are benign tumors that can grow in the uterus; they can be as big as a cantaloupe or as small as a pea. Ellen's was the size of a peach. During the C-section, the physicians not only realized the umbilical cord was wrapped around Stokely's little ankles, but he was also trapped by the fibroid. And Sadie was confined by the tumor too, so she had to be pulled out by her feet.

Here's the beautiful thing about all of what happened during my children's birth. There wasn't a male in the room except for me. The twins were brought into this world by women. Three black, female physicians performed the operation and delivered the babies. There were three nurses, nurse techs, and anesthesiologists for each child.

The birth wasn't easy for Ellen, but afterwards everything seemed fine. We were overjoyed to have two healthy babies. Stokely, who was a pound heavier than his tiny sister, looked eerily like my family. I could see my father, me, my nephew, and my brother stamped on his tiny face. Sadie didn't have that froggy look that babies sometimes have. She came out pursing her lips, with big beautiful eyes. Down South, if a newborn comes out a little homely, someone will say, "Oh bless her [or his] heart. She'll grow into her looks." But Sadie was undeniably gorgeous.

Shortly before 11 p.m., we sent everybody home. It was just me, Ellen, the twins, and the lactation nurse, who sat on one side of the bed, while I sat on the other. We were working on tandem breast feeding. While feeding the babies, Ellen started complaining of feeling hot and sleepy, so the nurse and I grabbed the babies, who were at each of her breasts. Ellen was growing faint and eventually passed out after violently throwing up. She woke up to me patting her head.

"Baby, you passed out and vomited. Are you okay?" I asked.

She was going in and out of consciousness. We put the babies in the bassinets and pressed the emergency button. I ran out into the hallway and shouted as loud and fiercely as I could, "Can we get some help for my wife?!"

Another nurse arrived, but I was steaming because I felt they were moving too slowly. I think many people in my shoes would have wanted them to move faster, no matter how fast they were moving.

I immediately FaceTimed Dr. Cannon, Ellen's primary OB/GYN, and also texted her. She was putting rollers in her hair but stopped everything to get back to the hospital.

Ellen would wake up to a room of activity. A white obstetrician, who happened to be our neighbor, was standing over her. "Your physicians are on the way. I heard the code over the intercom. I saw it was your room . . . Ellen, do you know who I am?" she asked.

"Yes," Ellen mumbled.

Within minutes, the whole critical care team was in the room, including the doctors who had conducted the C-section: Dr. Paige rushed in with an ultrasound machine; Dr. Cannon checked Ellen's bleeding and vitals; and Dr. Freeman examined her cervix.

The physicians decided they needed to go back into her uterus. "Are you sure?" Ellen asked. They were sure.

Ellen was wheeled out of the room in her bed, and Sadie, Stokely, and I stayed in the room. I pulled over the doctor's rolling chair and sat between their bassinets while I talked to them and fed them when I thought it was time.

A nurse brought me some formula and plastic nipples. I had to learn quick how to feed them and change their diapers. I called Nosizwe so that she could interpret what I might not understand. She had already made it home after being at the hospital for the births, but she was willing to turn around, despite living a ninety-minute drive away. She said she'd never heard that much fear in my voice before. I called my brother, too, who also came to the hospital. Nosizwe called Ellen's dad to let her family know what was happening. Two of Ellen's siblings also rushed to the hospital. For three or four hours, family members were downstairs and I was by myself with the babies upstairs—none of us knowing what was going on with Ellen.

My brother Lumumba sent me a text. "How are you holding up?"

"Scared."

"I'm going to step away and call you," he wrote.

My brother is the religious one, the minister in the family. "Make sure you are breathing," he said. "Everybody is depending on you at this moment. So be strong. You are the father, the husband, and you are running the show. You have to be strong."

That gave me the courage I needed to talk to Kai on the

phone throughout the night. She was terrified. "Is mom okay?" she kept asking.

I really didn't know what to tell her. But I said, "She's going to be okay."

"Please don't let anything happen to Mommy; Mommy means everything to me," she repeated.

That's when I broke down and cried. I tried not to, but I couldn't help myself. So Kai tried to comfort me. "It's going to be okay," she told me. It was a real role reversal for a thirteen-year-old.

As I waited to hear about my wife, I tended to our children. Every three hours I woke up to feed the babies, trying to put them to sleep, changing them, trying to figure out how to do everything. By the time Nosizwe arrived to be with us, I had somehow come up with a routine. She said I was just following instinct.

"Sadie is taking five milliliters of formula every three hours, but Stokely is taking seven and a half. I'm trying to get them to ten to twelve milliliters," I told her. "Sadie hasn't pooped yet, but Stokely has. He's already pooped three times."

My sister later said, "Bakari became a dad in two hours."

. .

Meanwhile, Ellen was still awake while taken into surgery. She told the doctors that she couldn't die because she had to live for her two new babies, for her daughter Kai, who desperately needed her, and for her husband. Three years earlier, Ellen's beloved brother had suddenly passed away. Even at the edge of death herself, she was thinking about her family, worried that her siblings and parents couldn't handle another sudden loss. And there was still so much she wanted to do in life.

The three physicians listened, held Ellen's hand, and prayed. Ellen told me that it was at that moment she knew why she had handpicked those doctors. She knew they not only cared and would listen to her, but they'd do whatever they could to save her life.

Ellen had earlier bonded over her love for getting her eyelashes extended with the female anesthesiologist, who walked into the room and said, "I hear you lost a few eyelashes." That made my wife laugh. She assured Ellen that she was in good hands. Ellen could hear the anesthesiologist ordering blood and telling people what to do and how fast she needed it done. Ellen was grateful for how seriously the doctor took everything, but she could also hear in the doctor's voice just how dire a situation it was. That's when she drifted off to sleep.

When the surgeons opened my wife up, they discovered that Ellen was bleeding out pretty good. Her blood had also started to clot in her uterus. The physicians pulled out clot after clot after clot. Ellen received seven units of blood; most people have only nine to twelve units in their entire body.

If we had been in Denmark, South Carolina, which no longer has a hospital, she surely would have died. Or if we had been in Orangeburg and she had to be transported to Charleston or Columbia, or if we had been in any other small rural county in a place like Alabama and had to get her air-lifted, she would not be here today.

The physicians inserted a device called a Bakri balloon that is used to control postpartum hemorrhage. Ellen believes that my quick call to her doctor and my shouting for help in the hallway helped save her life, and so, in her mind, it's not a coincidence that a balloon with a name similar to mine also saved her life. During her pregnancy, we took birth classes. The instructor always asked fathers what they were looking forward to, and I always said, "I'm just worried about my wife."

Ellen also worried. She once sat me down for a talk. "There will be times that it will be just me and you, and you have to be my advocate," she told me. "I will need you to be my advocate."

She now believes God was preparing us for war. We were both on heightened alert and took every precaution possible without anyone telling us to be so careful. She reminds me that when she fainted in the hospital room, I shouted loud enough to make everyone stop and listen.

Ellen woke up from surgery fighting, wanting to rip the ventilator out of her throat. For the next thirty-six hours, she was on life support. I went back and forth to be with my wife and then to be with our babies. Ellen recalled my kissing her and telling her that she needed to calm down. Despite her hands being in restraints, she got a pen from her friend Tara, who had come to be with me and the babies, and wrote, "This is a shit show" and "Tell them to take this thing out of my throat."

The medical team was surprised that she was so alert and able. "But I was determined," she later said. She was resolved to get to her family as soon as possible. When the doctors said she needed to be in the ICU for several days, she balked. She allowed us to bring the babies in an incubator only once to see her, worried they might get sick from the germs there. She also thought that Kai seeing her in that condition, swollen and in pain, would be too scary for her, so she insisted Kai visit only the babies.

Feeling nauseated after a dose of oxycodone, Ellen told the nurses to give her just Tylenol. She wanted to be fully aware of everything she was feeling, even her severe pain. She worried that if she fell asleep, she wouldn't wake up.

I continued to visit her in the ICU but tried not to be away from the babies for more than thirty minutes at a time. The hospital was very secure. Each parent needed to have a bracelet to move around, and a nurse or a parent had to be with the babies at all times.

Ellen was out of the ICU in only thirty-six hours. That was on Wednesday, January 9, 2019. We were able to leave for home two days later.

"I know that I was lucky," Ellen said. "I know that if one small detail in the chain of events had happened differently, I very likely would not be here to share my story. God gave me two miracle gifts on January 7, 2019, in the images of our twins, Stokely and Sadie. God also gave me a test, so I can share my testimony. I thank God every day that he spared my life that night because I have so much more life to live and so much work to do."

My wife and I are not upper class by any stretch. We live comfortably, but we are not wealthy. However, we can afford to find the physicians we want. And maybe that's even more important than the type of hospital or how many practitioners are looking out for you. We found doctors who looked like my wife, clearly understood her challenges, and cared deeply about her health.

All the doctors who helped my wife are people we know; we attend the same parties and circles. They were able to see what she was going through and understood her pain, understood that this wasn't normal and perceived the urgency to do what they needed to do. Because they knew us, they listened.

The idea of health equity is about meeting people where they are, providing them with quality care no matter their backgrounds. In our case, it was a matter of life or death. We were in the position to seek people out, to find people who not only looked like us but who listened to us. Most white people get this benefit because of privilege; most black people, regardless of socioeconomics, do not.

XI

Why 2016 Happened and the
Power of Rhetoric

This is an excerpt from my father's middle school book about South Carolina history:

There were more Negroes than whites in the state. The Negroes were uneducated, they had no knowledge of government, they did not know how to make a living without the supervision of the white man, they were so accustomed to being taken care of that they had no idea how to behave under freedom. They stole cattle and chickens and hogs, burned barns and stables. They were not willing to work. They were like children playing hooky the moment the teacher's back was turned. There were so many more Negroes than whites that they would have been in control if they had been allowed to vote. They nearly ruined the state during the years they voted.

The whites were determined this should not happen again. Regulations were made to prevent Negroes from voting. To this day, South Carolina is a white man's government.

It was written by Mary C. Simms Oliphant, the grand-daughter of southern slaveholder and author William Gilmore Simms. In the textbook excerpt, which Oliphant based on one of her grandfather's books from the 1860s, she's discussing the period after slavery and Reconstruction. Her work, for children, even justifies the existence of the Ku Klux Klan and why African Americans should not have the right to vote. Luckily, my father's African American teachers corrected the propaganda. Still, it's important to understand that many white teachers taught it as gospel to their students for decades, as late as the 1960s or later. If this type of warped history was being spread as fact about black people for hundreds of years and not so long ago, is it so difficult to understand why some white Americans still feel contempt toward African Americans?

. .

I never get caught up when people call me "nigger," and I'm called that a lot. The reason I don't let it bother me is something Stokely Carmichael said about racism and our reaction to it: "If a white man wants to lynch me, that's his problem, but if he's got the power to lynch me, that's my problem." So I don't get caught up in the sensationalized rhetoric or insults that people hurl at me. Instead, I focus on the people who have the power to implement systems of oppression.

During the 2016 election, on September 8, US presidential candidate Donald Trump did not like that I was expressing my support of Hillary Clinton on CNN, so he trolled me, tweeting, "@realDonaldTrump Henry McMaster, Lt. Governor of South Carolina who endorsed me, beat failed @CNN announcer Bakari Sellers so badly. Funny."

Then he blocked me, so there was no way for me to respond.

But I still slung a tweet back: "Temperament. If I can rattle you on @CNN, how can you handle Putin, @realDonaldTrump? 60 days out and worried about a kid from SC. Sad."

I find a big difference between that type of silly verbiage and Trump's dangerous rhetoric and actions of locking children in cages, trying to build a wall, straining and suffocating historically black colleges, and . . . of course, the list goes on. What really gets my attention are leaders who prevent their own citizens from having access to hospitals, decent schools, and clean water.

Despite Trump's criticism of my supporting Hillary, I get paid as a political commentator at CNN for my truth and for telling it through the lens of my life—political or otherwise.

I strongly believed Hillary could win the presidency in 2016. Like many people in this country, we imagined that at least white women would band with nonwhite voters to elect a woman over Trump, who had shown no evidence of having women's interests at heart.

During the election year, I was a surrogate for Hillary Clinton and became close to the former First Lady, US senator, and secretary of state. She traveled to speak at Denmark-Olar

Elementary School. Supporters packed the gymnasium to hear her vision for a subject dear to my heart: how to help blighted communities, like our rural towns in Bamberg County. The three hundred supporters, most of them African Americans, wanted to know whether Hillary could fix the Social Security system and bring them clean water. I told the media gathered that her visit proved there was more than one Flint, Michigan.

Hillary also invited me to speak at the Democratic National Convention, which I gratefully accepted. I was able to participate in that historical moment from a perch at CNN.

For political commentators, election night coverage is our Super Bowl. Before the big night, you're hoping to get the phone call from CNN execs that puts you up front with John King and the Magic Wall; with Wolf Blitzer, Jake Tapper, Dana Bash, and Anderson Cooper—there's nothing like it. That's what I wanted. I wanted to be a part of that Election Night Super Bowl when we had thirty million viewers.

I was excited and honored to get that phone call from CNN vice president Rebecca Kutler and was part of an email chain that set forth our schedule for Election Day. To be frank, everybody on set believed that Donald Trump was going to get destroyed. I predicted that Hillary Clinton would get 330 electoral votes, similar to Barack Obama's 2012 election, which was an electoral landslide.

The night before the election, I had spoken to Steve Schale, a political strategist and guru in Florida. He directed Obama's campaign in the Sunshine State in 2008 and returned in 2012 as senior adviser for Obama's Florida campaign. CNN's chief political analyst Gloria Borger had also spoken to him the night before. He told us both that he had run about thirteen simulations, and Hillary Clinton won in all but one. We were really confident going in.

Days before the election, I had received a call from one of Hillary's communications strategists, Adrienne Elrod, who told me, "The Secretary wants you to be at the Javits Center for a four-hour Election Night party. She would love it if you could be there. And she'd like to congratulate you and thank you on this night of celebration for all the great work you've done."

I knew I had to be on TV. I was on from 4 to 7 p.m., which means we'd be kicking off prime time. I wanted to be where history was being made, but I wanted to experience it through the media lens in Washington, DC, and on the set of CNN. Before I got back to the campaign to decline the invitation, I talked to Ellen and Kai. I wanted them to be with me on Election Day, but I also knew they were passionately excited about a woman leading the free world. There was a possibility they'd want to be in New York City with the president-elect; however, Ellen was fine with whatever I wanted to do, so I chose to stay with CNN.

There was hope during the night when Hillary won Virginia, and we knew she had the "blue wall" to depend on— states like Pennsylvania, Wisconsin, and Michigan—but when Trump chipped away at that blue wall, it became clear to me that things were not going well.

After my time on air, I was set to host a watch party at a club in DC. We snuck in Kai, who was then only ten years old, but I would do anything to make sure she was with me to watch the first woman become president of the United States. But, of course, that didn't happen. I felt I had let Kai down. I didn't want her to experience that type of disappointment, but she, like so many others, was so distraught. Ellen, Kai, and I left before the race was called and went back to our hotel room. I switched the TV off. I think the race wasn't called until 3:00 in the morning, but we were already asleep by 1 a.m.—I was already a few sheets to the wind, as they say, just trying to drink away my sorrows.

Kai woke up the next morning crying and worried that her tennis coach would be deported. She had a real fear because of the rhetoric, xenophobia, and bigotry that Donald Trump expressed. It filled a ten-year-old girl with terror. When I look back at that moment, it's emblematic of some of the larger fissures we have in our country.

The Myth

There's a direct and ugly line from Barack Obama to Donald Trump. The Obama era was a period of what *Slate* magazine's Jamelle Bouie described as a racial detente, or a temporary easing of racial hostilities, which subsided early in the Obama presidency but then boiled over into the election of Donald Trump. I bring this up because I want to dispel now and forever this so-called theory that voters in this country were economically anxious. I just don't believe that. It would take a whole hell of a lot of financial anxiety to be able to set aside a candidate's racism, bigotry, misogyny, and xenophobia. The overarching fear was not economic but cultural—the fear that somehow, black and brown people were going to replace whites. In 2042, the United States of America will be "majority minority," meaning that nonwhites will comprise the majority of US citizens, and that scares the shit out of some people. That's what's driving our current political discourse and rhetoric. Donald Trump speaks to those fears, and he pulled off the greatest con on Earth.

And yet, I don't believe voters are that stupid. I don't believe somebody who shits on a gold toilet can all of a sudden speak for what it means to be a factory worker or someone who toils on a farm every single day. I don't believe someone who started off with a multimillion-dollar loan from his father understands the plight of working-class Americans. Nor do I believe, by any stretch of the imagination, that all of Trump's supporters are racists; however, people were willing to set aside Trump's bigotry.

After the election of Barack Obama, there was talk of a postracial America. But in his 2017 farewell speech, Obama said that "such a vision, however well-intended, was never realistic. Race remains a potent and often divisive force in our society."

Obama won the presidency because he turned out a diverse electorate to build on existing Democratic turnout, and he was a once-in-a-generation political talent. Still, it's impossible to understand the past years, or the election of Trump, without fully grasping the prominent role of race in US politics.

Yes, racism has always been there, but a black president just damn near took the country over the edge politically. The toxicity surrounding Obama boiled over into our state politics. In South Carolina, political folks, including my friend Nikki Haley and my old opponent and now governor Henry McMaster, were unwilling to consider measures that literally would have kept white voters alive and kept all of our hospitals running. Medicaid expansion would have added four hundred thousand jobs in South Carolina and billions of dollars of revenue. But they, and virtually all other Republicans, were against it on the basis of their opposition to Obama's Affordable Care Act. Trump's win is a clear example of voters voting against their own self-interests. This is a not a new phenomenon, of course, but it's never been enough to win an election—until now.

Racism is deeply rooted in our politics, and in our political relationships, as my father's textbook demonstrates. Poor white people in South Carolina are not in any better position than poor black people—yet I'm not sure they understand that. My father often talks about an elderly white couple in Bamberg County who are so poor that they drive their lawnmower to the Piggly Wiggly grocery store—just like their black neighbors do. They prop a wooden board on the back of the mower so two can ride on it.

This couple is struggling like everyone else in the rural South. The fact that South Carolina is a deep red state makes it pretty likely that their friends and relatives will vote Republican, and have in the past, and therefore against policies that could help them eat and help them survive. But the legislators whom they choose vote against such policies because some people in certain political and media circles consider those policies to be geared toward helping only poor black people. How do poor whites square voting against their own interests?

My father believes that it all boils down to stereotypes and the alternate history South Carolinians have been taught to believe—that we black people didn't have a thing to do with building this country, that we are lazy and childlike, that we were treated kindly by slaveholders. Some people still to this day believe that the Civil War was not fought over slavery and that we nearly destroyed South Carolina during Reconstruction. Some writers have observed that South Carolina exists in a parallel universe. Well, just maybe that has something to do with miseducation.

Don't Be Selfish in Your Struggle

My grandmother always said, "You can't fall off the floor." It's one of those sayings from older people that you never fully understand when you're a kid. However, as time passes and you mature, you understand exactly what they were saying.

A lot of black folk have been on the floor with this gut punch of Donald Trump's election, but a lot of others are joining us down here: gay Americans, Muslim Americans, the disabled, and women of every race. The rural white poor are down here too, except they're just unreasonably expecting someone, Donald Trump, for instance, to help them up. So, we've been thrown to the floor—but now we can't fall, or be pushed, any lower.

The challenge is getting people to understand that we can't be selfish in our struggles. Yet a lot of my political allies, for some reason, are selfish.

I always tell people, you're never going to find anybody who believes in a woman's right to choose more than I do. I'll be out there on the front lines, marching; however, when another young black man is murdered in the streets, a man who looks like me, who doesn't get the benefit of his humanity, I expect those same white women I was marching with to march with me. This struggle against oppressive political power now requires accountability.

. .

I'd have to write another book to explore the issues surrounding race and religion. But if I did, I'd argue that one of the more disappointing narratives of this racial divide in our country has been the silence of white, male, Christian evangelicals. People may roll their eyes about this, but I firmly believe that in my relationship with God, I'm probably going to be in line ahead of Jerry Falwell Jr. and other evangelical heirs like Franklin Graham III as they try to get into heaven.

Why haven't these Christian leaders spoken up about the killings of black men by police? Why haven't they supported the #MeToo movement or railed against immigrant children being taken from their families? Why were they silent in the

aftermath of the 2017 white supremacist rally in Charlottesville, Virginia?

Race, religion, and power might be complicated, but ignor-
ing compassion is malpractice.

.   .

Barack Obama was way too cautious about race, and black folk
often got reactive measures that were insufficient for the oc-
casion. Unless you ask conservatives and many white people,
who often viewed Obama as siding with African Americans
over the police, the thorniest issue for Obama was the Black
Lives Matter movement. This movement, the police attacks it
was confronting, and the white resentment it precipitated are
partly attributed to Donald Trump's political victory. A great
deal of white frustration stemmed from the rise of Black Lives
Matter and Obama's tepid defense. I say, If you're going to go
in, go all in, because you're going to get blamed for it anyway.

Oftentimes, there's a group of people who have been yelling at the top of their lungs for a long time but who have gone
unheard. Back in the 1960s, some nameless civil rights protesters and marchers would carry signs that simply said, "I am a
man." Now we have a new wave of Black Lives Matter activists
who have reignited that passion for activism—not out of some
want, but out of pure necessity.

The question is, How many of us have to be murdered before someone does something? And if we wait on older Americans to do something, then the likelihood of it getting done
isn't high at all. It's an undeniable fact that black lives matter,

but some people like to say, "*All* lives matter." However, that's like saying at a breast cancer awareness rally that all cancer matters. It's true: all lives matter; but there's not a question about the value of police lives in this country or of white lives in this country. There *is* a question about the value of black lives—as there has been for about four hundred years.

Now, I may not be a card-carrying member of Black Lives Matter or an organizer for the movement, but I support them in everything they do. We have some disagreements about policy points and how things are done, but that's how protest movements are—they're messy.

A lot of my colleagues feel that activism must be accomplished outside the system. That's necessary for some, for sure, but I look at the Julian Bonds and the Andrew Youngs of the past and know I want to be an activist from within. And I'm not alone. There's Wes Bellamy, a city councilman in Charlottesville; Mandela Barnes, the lieutenant governor of Wisconsin; Michael Blake, a New York state assemblyman; and many others. There's Florida's Andrew Gillum and Georgia's Stacey Abrams. We're a new generation of activists, and we believe our task is to deconstruct these systems of oppression from within.

There are many people and groups who, rather than being the antitheses of each other, are attacking the virus of hatred and racism, oppression and bigotry, from different angles. It's all necessary. We would not have a Civil Rights Act and a Voting Rights Act today if we hadn't had a black power movement and a Southern Christian Leadership Conference, and everything and everyone in between. Why attack from all fronts?

Because you can't merely protest in the streets without policy initiatives. It doesn't matter if you're chanting "I can't breathe" to protest the death of Eric Garner if the police are not held accountable, legislatively and under the law.

So what do I want? I want the same thing my father wanted. I want what all of my "aunts" and "uncles" who were part of the civil rights movement wanted.

I want freedom.

What does that look like? Freedom from discrimination, including at the ballot box. Freedom from violence—from the domestic terrorism that took Clem Pinckney to the violence at the hands of police, who killed unarmed black folk like Michael Brown, Eric Garner, Keith Lamont Scott, and Walter Scott. Freedom to live in communities where our children are not drinking water that contains lead, communities that have hospitals and safe neighborhoods. I want us to live up to our potential, which means equal schools, economic opportunity, and entrepreneurship.

Our challenge is broader than that of my dad's generation. His generation was focused on equal access; they wanted to empower their communities economically, politically, and socially—but they also wanted to sit at the same lunch counters, drink from the same water fountains, go to the same schools.

I want this country I love to atone for slavery, for Jim Crow, for the prison-industrial complex, and for the attitude of ambivalence toward state violence against unarmed black men.

Like my father, and his father, and—I don't doubt—his father too: we all deserve to be free and equal.

Their Eyes Are Watching

We're not sure where Stokely and Sadie get their large eyes from. When they look at you, it's like they're peering into your soul. Maybe their wise gazes come from them entering this world fighting, overcoming, and now they're just watching for their mom and dad to make their next move.

After my wife barely survived their birth in January 2019, we were all able to go home, but the visceral terror of our next chapter had only begun to unravel. Ellen and I watched Sadie die a little bit every day. Sadie was born with biliary atresia, a rare condition in infants. Simply put, it's a disease of the bile ducts and liver. The illness strikes about 1 out of 12,000 babies in the nation.

The first year of Sadie's life was brutal on all of us, but she's strong, just like Ellen. I find it sadly poetic that Sadie's mother would wrestle for her life to ensure our two babies got here and that little Sadie would work just as hard to make sure she stayed. Stokely, my boy, is strong in his own way. Because we had to pick up and move, he was without us for a long period of time. Meanwhile, Sadie got sicker, but there was nothing we could do. There were nights when Ellen would ask, "Did God give us this baby just to take her away?" We were questioning faith and doctors—we were questioning everything. But in the end, all we had was God, our faith, and the good physicians at Duke University.

We waited and waited for a transplant. It was my job to make sure Ellen could make it day by day. Sadie's belly got really big, she was so thin, and her skin turned yellow. Those months of waiting were pure hell.

We were on the donor's list for ninety-three days. Each day was extremely difficult because we were watching our daughter die. As fate would have it on Friday, August 30, I received a frantic call from my niece, Skyla, with my wife wailing in the background. Ellen's father, Dr. Rucker, had just died. They found him on his tractor. He was clearing rocks and boulders in the woods, preparing for deer hunting season. He had a massive heart attack, literally dying doing what he loves. So I rushed out and drove an hour and a half home. I called my brother and sister, who came to the house as well. Ellen eventually traveled to Lancaster to be with her family, but I stayed with the twins. Kai was her mother's protector. While I was with Sadie and Stokely, she took care of Ellen.

On the same day, Ellen called to say that Duke had contacted her to say they had a liver. I told her not to get excited because sometimes it's a dry run, and it ends up not really working. I said let's just keep doing what we have to do. We packed the car on Sunday and drove to Duke. We were at the hospital all day preparing for the transplant. We knew when the liver arrived because we could hear the helicopter land. The entire process was so fascinating. At the time of the surgery, everything is timed out. So Sadie is open, her liver is out, and the other liver is also there, ready to be put into her. There's not a second to be wasted. It's excruciating. Our little girl is having a transplant and I'm just sitting there nervous with my wife, but Ellen wasn't nervous. Her mind was occupied with planning her father's funeral. After the transplant, I told Ellen to go back to Lancaster to grieve with her family; I stayed three days at the hospital with Sadie. Several days later, Vince Carter would play an important role. He was with Kai before and after the funeral, which was on September 7. Our family might be nontraditional, but we are always there for one another.

After we watched Sadie come back alive after receiving a transplant, we wanted to make sure treatment is accessible to all children suffering from liver disease, so we established the Sadie Ellen Sellers Fund at Duke Children's Hospital.

Today, Sadie gives you open-mouth kisses and runs around the house. She's very vocal, but Stokely talks even more. He'll tell you exactly how he feels, and Sadie will follow her brother, laughing the entire time.

She overcame her illness, and it's my job to ensure she doesn't have to overcome injustices. Now that Ellen and I are parents of three black children in Trump's America we must get to the work of changing the world. It's our job to help deconstruct the systems of oppression that have consumed the lives of many African Americans. It's a challenge that has become very real for us as we watch our children grow before our eyes. We don't want Sadie and Stokely to live in a world where there's only dirty water to drink or where there are no hospitals. To be very blunt and honest, I don't want Sadie or Kai to end up like Sandra Bland, or Stokely like Philando Castile. I want them to be able to live to their full potential. I want them to realize there is a crown above their head.

Ellen and I have a big challenge ahead of us. The repercussions of Trump won't end in four years—it will be with us forever. The country will need a complete exorcism. Like my mother says, "We are going to need some sage."

I was thinking about my children's future while being interviewed by CNN's John Berman about Sadie's transplant. I imagined clearing a path for my daughter, who I hope and believe will grow up to have her finger on the trigger of her own future.

"Those ninety days were hell," I told Berman. "So now we are just paving a way for Sadie to become the next president of the United States."

Dear Donor Family,

We are writing to express our sincerest gratitude. Words cannot truly do just for the appreciation we have for your family. Our Sadie was very ill and in desperate need of a new liver. Your family member gave our little girl the gift of life.

Sadie is a twin and was born with a rare disease called biliary atresia. She was sick her entire life until her liver transplant. We agonized for ninety-three days on the waiting list just being prayerful and hopeful. On August 30, our lives changed in so many ways. The patriarch of our family, Sadie's grandfather, who was not sick, died at around 9 a.m. that morning, and at 5 p.m. that evening our daughter's doctors called and said that there was a liver for our little girl.

We know that this time in your lives is very painful, and we could never truly understand that pain. We are so sorry for your loss. Please know that we will honor your family and be forever grateful for the gift that you have given our little girl. Her life was saved because of you. For that, our hearts are full of thanks.

Thank you!

ACKNOWLEDGMENTS

My Vanishing Country is a true labor of love for me, and it could not have been done without the support, encouragement, and faith of so many people. It would be impossible to name them all, though I must start with my kin. I do not have a large family, but my mother and father are my heroes, my true North Stars. They did whatever necessary to ensure I had the tools growing up to try to reach my greatest aspirations. Nosizwe and Lumumba, my sister and brother, have always been there for me, even as we try to navigate the expectations of life and simply make our parents proud. Although they are gone, I owe great thanks to my grandparents for giving so much through the ministry, military, business, and classroom. Their lessons of service to community provided me with a playbook on how to give as well as a reason to stand tall and be proud.

I truly believe I'm a child of "The Movement." For all those who have sacrificed and bled for the freedoms we have today— this is an ode to you.

"Friendship" is an overused word, but the contributions of Jamil "Pop" Williams, Jarrod Loadholt, Brandon Childs,

Brian Fitch, Jason Mercer, Rob Hewitt, and Anthony Locke cannot be understated. As we grow into fathers and husbands, I hope one day you will reach for this book, dust it off a bit, and show your children through these pages how we all have grown from boys to men.

I also owe a tremendous debt of gratitude to HarperCollins and my team. I knocked on the doors of twenty publishers, who I hoped would listen to my ideas, but to no avail. However, Tracy Sherrod, Judith Curr, and Patrik Henry Bass not only took my call but invited me to come to their offices in New York City to sell myself and my story. To Paul Fedorko, Tatsha Robertson, and Crystal Johns, you never gave up on me, and through all the frustrations, we have created a book that I hope can impact the lives of many for generations to come. Thank you, Jeff Ourvan, for your careful reads.

My four years at Morehouse College cultivated me into the man I am today. It was Morehouse that placed that crown above my head and challenged me to continue working and growing to one day reach it.

Lastly, these are the most emotional sentences of the entire book. Ellen, I love you so much. You are everything and my true partner. You giving me the strength daily to get through life's challenges allowed me to pour my heart out on paper. Kai, Stokely, and Sadie, I will give my all every day so that you can be free. Daddy loves you.

ABOUT THE AUTHOR

Bakari Sellers is a CNN political analyst and was the youngest-ever member of the South Carolina state legislature. Named in 2010 to *Time* magazine's "40 Under 40" list, he is also a practicing attorney fighting to give a voice to the voiceless.